YOUR recip[e] could appea[r] in our next cookbook!

Share your tried & true family favorites with us instantly at

www.gooseberrypatch.com

If you'd rather jot 'em down by hand, just mail this form to...

Gooseberry Patch • Cookbooks – Call for Recipes
PO Box 812 • Columbus, OH 43216-0812

If your recipe is selected for a book, you'll receive a FREE copy!

Please share only your original recipes or those that you have made your own over the years.

Recipe Name:

Number of Servings:

Any fond memories about this recipe? Special touches you like to add or handy shortcuts?

Ingredients (include specific measurements):

Instructions (continue on back if needed):

Special Code: **cookbookspage**

Over

Extra space for recipe if needed:

Tell us about yourself...

Your complete contact information is needed so that we can send you your FREE cookbook, if your recipe is published. Phone numbers and email addresses are kept private and will only be used if we have questions about your recipe.

Name:

Address:

City: State: Zip:

Email:

Daytime Phone:

Thank you! Vickie & Jo Ann

5-Ingredient
Family Favorite
RECIPES

325 quick-fix recipes for any occasion,
plus time-saving tips and hints.

Gooseberry Patch

An imprint of Globe Pequot
64 South Main Street
Essex, CT 06426

www.gooseberrypatch.com

1•800•854•6673

Copyright 2024, Gooseberry Patch 978-1-62093-581-1

Do you have a tried & true recipe...

tip, craft or memory that you'd like to see featured in
a **Gooseberry Patch** cookbook? Visit our website at
www.gooseberrypatch.com and follow the
easy steps to submit your favorite family recipe.
Or send them to us at:

Gooseberry Patch
PO Box 812
Columbus, OH 43216-0812

Don't forget to include the number of servings your recipe makes,
plus your name, address, phone number and email address. If we
select your recipe, your name will appear right along with it...
and you'll receive a **FREE** copy of the book!

Contents

Dedication

For everyone who loves sitting down to a good home-cooked meal with family...but doesn't want to spend all day making it!

Appreciation

*We can't count the ways we appreciate all of our **Gooseberry Patch** friends who generously shared your best recipes with us!*

SIMPLE
Soups & Breads

Hamburger Vegetable Soup

Katie Larrabee
Elmira Heights, NY

This is a versatile recipe that can easily be changed up to suit the tastes of your family. Use ground turkey or chicken, if you like... choose your family's favorite veggies. It's always good.

1 to 2 lbs. ground beef
1 to 2 32-oz. containers beef,
   chicken or vegetable broth
15-oz. can diced tomatoes

15-oz. can diced potatoes,
   drained and rinsed
1 to 2 10-oz. pkgs. frozen
   mixed vegetables

In a large stockpot, brown beef over medium heat; drain. Add broth, tomatoes with juice and remaining ingredients; bring to a boil. Reduce heat to medium-low. Simmer for 15 to 20 minutes, stirring occasionally, until heated through. Makes 6 to 8 servings.

Zucchini-Beef Soup

Lynnette Jones
East Flat Rock, NC

My mother-in-law used to make this delicious soup for us.

1 lb. ground beef
1 t. garlic salt
1 t. pepper

3/4 c. onion, chopped
2 to 3 zucchini, sliced or diced
28-oz. can crushed tomatoes

Brown beef in a soup pot over medium heat. Drain; season with garlic salt and pepper. Add onion and cook until tender. Stir in zucchini and tomatoes with juice; reduce heat to medium-low. Simmer for about one hour, stirring occasionally. Makes 8 servings.

Just 5 ingredients...that's all it takes to make these quick & tasty recipes! Our ground rules...water, salt and pepper don't count as ingredients (you've already got those!), nor do optional ingredients and garnishes. Now, let's get cooking!

Soups & Breads

Chicken & Stars Soup

Lynn Williams
Muncie, IN

An easy warm-you-up soup to make for chilly days. My kids love it when I use alphabet noodles instead of stars.

8 c. chicken broth
16-oz. pkg. frozen mixed
   vegetables

2 c. cooked chicken, diced
1 c. tiny star pasta, uncooked
salt and pepper to taste

Bring broth to a boil in a large stockpot over high heat. Add frozen vegetables; reduce heat to medium and simmer for about 15 minutes. Stir in chicken and pasta; cook until pasta is tender, about 10 minutes. Season with salt and pepper. Serves 6 to 8.

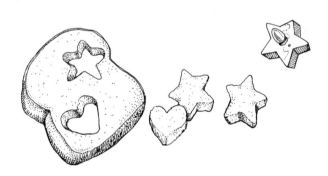

Use mini cookie cutters to make whimsical soup croutons...
kids will love them! Cut out fun shapes from slices of day-old bread,
brush with butter and bake at 200 degrees until croutons
are crunchy and golden.

Mémère Soup

Linda Richard
Bangor, ME

My French-Canadian mother was called "Mémère" by her grandchildren. She always used leftover chicken and whatever pasta she had left in the cupboard, or even rice. My niece came up with the name "Mémère Soup" because we had no name for it! That was over 45 years ago, and we still make it to this day. Any leftovers are delicious the next day.

8 c. water
1/2 c. elbow macaroni, mini
   shell pasta or broken
   spaghetti pieces, uncooked

1/2 c. onion, chopped
salt and pepper to taste
2 to 3 c. cooked chicken, diced
28-oz. can crushed tomatoes

In a stockpot, bring water to a boil over high heat. Add pasta, onion, salt and pepper. Cook for 10 minutes, or until pasta is tender. Reduce heat to medium-low; stir in chicken and tomatoes with juice. Simmer until heated through, stirring occasionally. Serves 4 to 6.

Frozen chopped onions are especially good time-savers for soups, casseroles or one-dish dinners. Simply substitute the frozen onions for the same amount of fresh in your recipe. As a bonus...no more tears while slicing onions!

SIMPLE
Soups & Breads

Cheesy Corn Chowder

Beth Richter
Canby, MN

I make this yummy soup often. It's definitely a comfort food that warms me up when it's cold outside, but it tastes so good that I sometimes make it in warm weather too. If you wish, use a package of frozen corn, cooked and drained, instead of the canned corn.

10-3/4 oz. can cream of
    mushroom soup
1-1/4 c. milk
2 11-oz. cans corn, drained

10 slices American cheese
2.8-oz. can Cheddar or plain
    French fried onions

Whisk together soup and milk in a saucepan over medium-low heat. Stir in corn; heat through but do not boil. Add cheese slices and stir into the soup until melted. Ladle soup into bowls; garnish with onions. Serves 4.

Beer Bread Biscuits

Mertie Stardevant
Washington, NC

This simple recipe is from my sister-in-law. It's a hit every time we have soup!

2 c. biscuit baking mix
3 T. sugar

12-oz. can regular or
    non-alcoholic beer

Combine all ingredients in a bowl; mix well. Spoon batter into greased muffin cups, filling 3/4 full. Bake at 325 degrees for 20 minutes. Makes 6 to 8 biscuits.

Keep fresh-baked bread warm and toasty! Slip a piece of aluminum foil into the bread basket, then top it with a decorative napkin.

Spicy Potato-Beef Soup

Suzan Mechling
Round Rock, TX

I was born and raised in Ohio before we moved to Texas several years ago. This was such a quick & easy soup to make on a cold day.

1 lb. ground beef
4 c. potatoes, peeled and cubed
1/2 c. onion, chopped
3 8-oz. cans tomato sauce
4 c. water
1/2 to 1 t. hot pepper sauce
2 t. salt
1-1/2 t. pepper

In a Dutch oven or large kettle, brown beef over medium heat; drain. Add remaining ingredients; bring to a boil. Reduce heat to medium-low. Simmer for one hour, stirring occasionally, or until potatoes are tender and soup has thickened. Makes 6 to 8 servings.

Erica's Chip Dip Soup

Heidi Kaufman
Fort Wayne, IN

Put away the spoons for this zesty soup and use tortilla chips instead, like we do! At the end of an especially long and trying day, my dear friend Erica made this dinner for me. It has been brightening days in my house ever since.

1 lb. ground beef
16-oz. pkg. frozen corn
16-oz. jar favorite salsa
8-oz. pkg. cream cheese, cubed
Garnish: tortilla chips

Brown beef in a large saucepan over medium heat; drain. Add frozen corn; cook until corn is heated through. Stir in salsa. Cook and stir until cream cheese is completely melted and blended in. Serve with tortilla chips. Serves 4 to 6.

A delicious way to use leftover roast beef...chop or shred and use instead of ground beef in your favorite soup recipe.

Creamy Potato Soup

Julie Pak
Henryetta, OK

This soup just soothes the soul! It's delicious served with cornbread, hot rolls or even crackers. My mom made this a lot when I was a kid. We always loved it when it was chilly outside or we didn't feel well.

6 potatoes, peeled and diced
1 bunch green onions or
    1 yellow onion, diced
2 T. butter

salt and pepper to taste
12-oz. can evaporated milk
1/4 c. cold water
1 T. cornstarch

Combine potatoes and onions in a stockpot. Add enough water to cover vegetables by one inch. Add butter, salt and pepper; bring to a boil over medium heat. Simmer until vegetables are tender, 15 to 20 minutes. Season with more salt and pepper, if desired. Stir in evaporated milk. In a cup, stir cold water into cornstarch until dissolved; stir into soup. Simmer for 5 more minutes, or until thickened. Makes 6 servings.

For thick, creamy vegetable soup, use a hand-held immersion blender to purée some of the cooked veggies right in the saucepan. Works great with potato or bean soup too.

Harvest Clam Chowder

Julie Ann Perkins
Anderson, IN

This hearty made-from-scratch chowder is delicious. It can be stirred up in just a few minutes, so why not try it?

2 T. butter
1/4 c. onion, chopped
Optional: 1/4 c. celery, chopped
1 c. potatoes, peeled and diced

1 c. heavy cream
2 c. canned minced clams
  with juice
salt and pepper to taste

Melt butter in a large saucepan over medium heat. Add onion and celery, if using; sauté until golden. Add potatoes and cook until tender. Stir in cream and clams with juice. Heat through but do not boil. Makes 3 to 4 servings.

Boston Brown Bread

Lynda Robson
Boston, MA

We used to love it when my grandmother baked little loaves in empty cans for us. I still do it now & then. Just grease the cans well, fill a bit more than half full, set cans on a baking sheet and bake at 350 degrees for 25 to 30 minutes. They make great gifts!

2 c. whole-wheat flour
1 c. all-purpose flour
1 t. baking soda
1/4 t. salt

1-1/2 c. buttermilk
1 c. molasses
Optional: 2/3 c. raisins
  or currants

Stir together flours, baking soda and salt in a large bowl. Add buttermilk and molasses; mix well. Fold in raisins or currants, if using. Pour batter into a greased 9"x5" loaf pan. Bake at 375 degrees for one hour, until a toothpick inserted into center of loaf tests clean. Makes one loaf.

Homestyle tomato soup for two...just right for sharing on a rainy day! Combine a can of tomato soup with a can of diced tomatoes and simmer until hot. Add a little Italian seasoning and a splash of milk, if you like it creamy.

SIMPLE
Soups & Breads

Quick Crab Chowder

John Alexander
New Britain, CT

Mmm...I can almost smell the ocean when I serve this soup!
I like to add a sprinkle of parsley or paprika and serve with
a basket of saltine crackers.

2 russet potatoes, peeled
   and cubed
2 c. milk
1 c. half-and-half

1 c. canned lump crabmeat,
   drained
4 green onions, sliced
salt and pepper to taste

In a soup pot, cover potatoes with water; bring to a boil over high heat. Cook potatoes until fork-tender, about 15 minutes; drain. Add milk and half-and-half; mash potatoes well with a potato masher or fork. Gently stir in remaining ingredients. Cook over low heat until heated through and slightly thickened, 3 to 5 minutes. Serves 4.

Bread bowls make a hearty soup extra special. Cut the tops off round bread loaves and hollow out, then rub with olive oil and garlic. Pop in the oven at 400 degrees for 10 minutes, or until crusty and golden. Ladle in soup and serve right away.

Creamy Chicken Noodle Soup

Marian Forck
Chamois, MO

When you just aren't feeling the best, this soup will hit the spot.
When you're feeling fine, it's even better!

8 c. water
8 cubes chicken bouillon
6-1/2 c. wide egg noodles,
   uncooked
2 10-3/4 oz. cans cream of
   chicken soup

3 c. cooked chicken, cubed
8-oz. container sour cream
Optional: shredded Cheddar
   cheese, chopped fresh
   parsley

In a large saucepan over high heat, bring water and bouillon to a boil; stir until bouillon dissolves. Add noodles and cook until tender, about 10 minutes. Do not drain. Reduce heat to medium. Stir in soup and chicken; heat through. Remove from heat; stir in sour cream. If desired, top servings with cheese and parsley. Makes 10 to 12 servings.

Apple-Raisin Muffins

Liz Plotnick-Snay
Gooseberry Patch

A basket of fresh-baked muffins turns a bowl of soup into
a meal! Serve warm with lots of butter.

9-oz. pkg. apple-cinnamon
   muffin mix
2 T. milk
1 egg, beaten

1 c. Gala or Golden Delicious
   apple, peeled and grated
1/2 c. raisins

Combine muffin mix, milk and egg in a large bowl; stir until well moistened. Fold in fruit. Spoon batter into greased muffin cups, filling 2/3 full. Bake at 400 degrees for 20 to 25 minutes. Makes 6 to 8 muffins.

For juicy, flavorful chicken, cover with water and simmer gently until cooked through, then turn off the heat and let the chicken cool in its own broth.

SIMPLE
Soups & Breads

Pantry Tomato Soup

Christina Sheppard,
Centerville, OH

Serve with grilled cheese sandwiches for a simply splendid lunch.

14-1/2 oz. can diced tomatoes
    with basil, garlic and
    oregano
28-oz. can tomato sauce

14-1/2 oz. can tomato soup
14-1/2 oz. can chicken broth
Garnish: sour cream, grated
    Parmesan cheese,
    fish-shaped crackers

Combine undrained tomatoes, sauce, soup and broth in a slow cooker.
Cover and cook on low setting for 2 hours, or until heated through.
Garnish as desired. Serves 6 to 8.

There's nothing cozier than tomato soup and grilled cheese.
Make your sandwiches even tastier...before grilling, spread
the bread with mayonnaise instead of butter.

Susan's Red Lentil & Cauliflower Soup

Linda Galvin
Ames, IA

My friend Susan has a lot of dietary restrictions. She and I like this simple recipe for a quick meal. This soup is not only gluten and dairy-free but vegetarians would enjoy as well.

1 c. dried red lentils, rinsed
4 c. water
1/2 c. mild, medium or hot salsa

Optional: 1 onion, chopped
salt to taste
2 c. cauliflower, chopped

In a large saucepan over medium-high heat, combine lentils, water, salsa and onion, if using. Bring to a boil. Reduce heat to medium-low and simmer for 10 minutes. Add cauliflower; continue simmering another 10 minutes, or until tender. Serves 2 to 3.

If the soup tastes a little flat, perk it up with a little lemon or lime juice, or plain or flavored vinegar. Add just a teaspoon and taste, then add a little more as needed. A bouillon cube or two can also do the trick.

White Bean & Pesto Soup

JoAnn
Gooseberry Patch

Earthy, satisfying and takes no time at all to make!
Serve with a hot loaf of crusty bread.

3 15-1/2 oz. cans cannellini
    beans, drained and rinsed
2-1/2 to 3 c. chicken broth,
    divided
1/4 c. shredded Parmesan
    cheese, divided

8 to 10 sun-dried tomatoes in
    water, drained and sliced
1/3 c. pesto sauce
salt and pepper to taste

In a large saucepan, combine beans and 1-1/2 cups broth. Bring to a boil over medium-high heat. Reduce heat to medium-low. Simmer for 8 to 10 minutes, until thickened. Stir in 3 tablespoons cheese and remaining ingredients; add remaining broth to desired consistency. Heat through, but do not boil. Garnish with remaining cheese. Makes 6 servings.

Cheddar-Olive Bread Sticks

Dale Duncan
Waterloo, IA

These are tasty served with soup or as an appetizer.

2-1/4 c. biscuit baking mix
2/3 c. milk
1/2 c. shredded Cheddar cheese
1/3 c. pimento-stuffed green
    olives, chopped

1 egg, beaten
Garnish: olive oil or marinara
    sauce

In a large bowl, stir together baking mix, milk, cheese and olives until a soft dough forms. Remove dough to a floured surface; gently roll in flour to coat. Shape into a ball; knead 10 times. Divide dough into 3 balls; divide each ball into 5 equal pieces. Shape each into a roll about 8 inches long. Arrange on 2 lightly greased baking sheets. Brush dough with beaten egg. Bake at 350 degrees for 11 to 14 minutes, until lightly golden. Serve warm with olive oil or marinara sauce for dipping. Makes 15 bread sticks.

Potato-Corn Chowder

Susan Church
Holly, MI

A creamy comfort soup good for a cool crisp day.
Great paired up with crusty French bread.

4 potatoes, peeled and chopped
3 c. water
1 c. onion, chopped
1-1/2 t. butter

12-oz. can evaporated skim milk
14-1/2 oz. can cream-style corn
1 t. salt
1/4 t. pepper

In a large saucepan over high heat, cook potatoes in water until tender; do not drain. Meanwhile, in a skillet over medium heat, sauté onion in butter until tender and translucent. Add onion mixture, milk, corn and seasonings to potato mixture. Cook over medium-low heat for 25 to 30 minutes, stirring occasionally. Makes 8 servings.

O'Brien-Style Potato Soup

Brenda Hughes
Houston, TX

I make this a day ahead...it's always best the second day. So easy with very few ingredients. Frozen hashbrowns that already include the peppers and onions save chopping time!

28-oz. pkg. frozen diced
   hashbrowns with onions
   and peppers
3 14-oz. cans chicken broth

2-3/4 oz. pkg. peppered white
   gravy mix
1/2 c. half-and-half

Combine potatoes, broth and gravy mix in a stockpot over medium heat. Bring to a boil, stirring often. Reduce heat to low; simmer for 20 minutes. Stir in half-and-half. Simmer over low heat for 10 to 15 minutes, but do not boil. Soup will gradually thicken. Serve immediately, or cover, refrigerate overnight and rewarm to serve the next day. Makes 6 servings.

Separate frozen vegetables in a jiffy...place them in a colander and run under cold water.

Broccoli-Wild Rice Soup

*Marian Forck
Chamois, MO*

Feeling the blues? This soup will perk you right up.

7 c. water
6-oz. pkg. chicken & wild
  rice mix
10-3/4 oz. can cream of
  chicken soup
16-oz. pkg. frozen chopped
  broccoli

4 carrots, peeled and sliced
2 T. onion, finely chopped
Optional: 1 c. cooked chicken,
  cubed
Garnish: 3-oz. pkg. slivered
  almonds

In a large soup pot over high heat, combine water with rice mix and seasoning packet. Bring to a boil. Reduce heat to medium-low; cover and simmer for 10 minutes, stirring once. Stir in soup, broccoli, carrots, onion and chicken, if using. Simmer for 25 minutes, stirring occasionally. Stir in almonds just before serving. Makes 5 to 6 servings.

Janie's 5-Can Soup

*Julie Bayless
Burleson, TX*

I got this recipe from my friend Janie, who had big, hungry boys to feed. It is so easy and yummy. I try to keep the ingredients in my pantry so it's ready to make on busy days. Great with tortilla chips and Cheddar cheese on top too.

15-oz. can ranch-style beans
14-3/4 oz. can creamed corn
10-3/4 oz. can chicken &
  rice soup

10-can diced tomatoes with
  green chiles
13-oz. can cooked chicken

Combine all ingredients in a large saucepan; do not drain. Simmer over medium-low heat until bubbly and heated through. Makes 8 servings.

A permanent marker makes it a snap to keep food cans rotated in the pantry. Just write the purchase date on each item as groceries are unpacked.

Slow-Cooked Bean Soup

Stephanie Mayer
Portsmouth, VA

If you have a holiday ham bone left over, add it to this easy soup, for even more delicious flavor.

4-1/2 c. frozen onion, celery
    and carrot mix
8-3/4 c. chicken broth, divided
16-oz. pkg. dried bean soup mix
2 T. tomato paste

1 t. salt
1/2 t. pepper
14-1/2 oz. can petite diced
    Italian-seasoned tomatoes

In a large skillet over medium heat, sauté vegetable mix in 1/4 cup broth until tender. Transfer vegetables to a 6-quart slow cooker; add remaining broth, bean soup mix, tomato paste and seasonings. Cover and cook on low setting for 8 to 10 hours. Stir in tomatoes with juice; turn setting to high. Cover and cook about 15 minutes longer. Serves 10 to 12.

Homemade soup is a great way to use up those odds & ends in the fridge. Leftover veggies, cooked rice and even a bit of tomato paste or pesto can be added to make a new and delicious soup.

SIMPLE
Soups & Breads

Homestyle Cabbage Soup

*Aleta Whitford
Greenville, IL*

*I like to make a double batch of this soup and freeze it
in single servings to take to work. Sometimes I garnish it with
crumbled bacon or shredded cheese...yummy!*

1 head cabbage, shredded
1 onion, thinly sliced
1 to 2 potatoes, peeled and
   thinly sliced

2 c. skim milk
2 T. margarine
salt and pepper to taste
1 c. water

Combine cabbage, onion and potatoes in a heavy saucepan with a
small amount of water. Cover and cook over medium-low heat until
tender. Mash cabbage to a pulp, leaving a little with some texture. Stir
in remaining ingredients. Simmer over low heat for 10 to 15 minutes.
Serves 4 to 6.

Quick Cheese Biscuits

*Kerry Mayer
Dunham Springs, LA*

*At my house, hot bread is a must at dinnertime. This recipe
is so easy that my daughter often helps.*

2 c. biscuit baking mix
2/3 c. milk
2/3 c. shredded Cheddar cheese

1/4 c. butter, melted
1 t. garlic powder

In a bowl, combine baking mix, milk and cheese; mix well. Drop batter
by heaping tablespoonfuls onto a lightly greased baking sheet. Bake at
450 degrees for 8 to 10 minutes. Combine butter and garlic powder;
brush over hot biscuits when they come out of the oven. Makes
1-1/2 dozen.

Canned and frozen vegetables are a
snap to swap in soup recipes. Just
allow enough simmering time for
frozen veggies to cook through.

Zesty Sausage & Bean Chili

Lily Northup
Sheldon, IA

I wanted to make my own chili and came up with this yummy slow-cooker recipe. It's a big hit with the kids! Serve it up with shredded cheese, sour cream or your own favorite toppings...and cornbread, of course! You can add more sausage and beans as you wish too.

1 lb. ground pork sausage,
   browned and drained
3 15-1/2 oz. cans chili beans
   in chili sauce

14-1/2 oz. can zesty chili-style
   diced tomatoes
1-oz. pkg. chili seasoning mix
Optional: 8-oz. can tomato sauce

Combine all ingredients except tomato sauce in a 5-quart slow cooker; do not drain beans and tomatoes. Stir until well mixed. Cover and cook on low setting for 6 hours. If more liquid is needed, add tomato sauce. Makes 8 servings.

Southwestern Flatbread

Rita Morgan
Pueblo, CO

Yum...hot fresh-baked bread to enjoy with your soup! Easy to change up to Italian flavors too, with oregano and Parmesan cheese.

2 t. olive oil, divided
11-oz. tube refrigerated crusty
   French loaf

1/2 c. roasted sunflower kernels
1 t. chili powder
1/2 to 1 t. coarse salt

Brush a 15"x10" jelly-roll pan with one teaspoon oil; unroll dough onto pan. Use a floured rolling pin to roll out into a rectangle. Drizzle dough with remaining oil; brush over dough. In a small bowl, combine sunflower kernels and chili powder; mix well and sprinkle over dough. Firmly press kernels into dough; sprinkle with salt. Bake at 375 degrees for 12 to 16 minutes, until golden. Remove flatbread to a wire rack; cool 10 minutes. Tear or cut into pieces. Makes about 15 pieces.

SIMPLE
Soups & Breads

Taco Chili with a Twist

Annette Thomas
Huntsville, AL

My kids love eating this chili with tortilla chips or cornbread. You can use leftover taco beef from the night before or even make a big batch of beef and freeze half for later. I have used all sorts of canned beans, whatever I have on hand.

1 lb. ground beef
1-oz. pkg. taco seasoning mix
4 16-oz. cans assorted beans
   like Great Northern, pinto,
   kidney, chili and/or
   pork & beans

14-3/4 oz. can creamed corn
16-oz. bottle cocktail vegetable
   juice
Optional: shredded Cheddar
   cheese

Brown beef in a skillet over medium heat; drain. Stir in taco seasoning; transfer beef to a 6-quart slow cooker. Add beans, draining all except chili beans and pork & beans. Stir in corn. Add enough vegetable juice to fill slow cooker to within 2 inches of the top. Cover and cook on high setting for one to 2 hours, or on low setting for 3 to 4 hours, until heated through. Top with cheese, if desired. Serves 8.

The most indispensable ingredient of all good home cooking: love for those you are cooking for.
– Sophia Loren

23

Slow-Cooker White Chicken Chili

Nancy Lanning
Lancaster, SC

While our daughter was babysitting a family, they served white chili. It has now become a favorite of our family too!

48-oz. jar Great Northern beans
16-oz. jar mild, medium or
   hot salsa
1/2 t. garlic, minced

2-1/2 c. cooked chicken,
   chopped
16-oz. pkg. mozzarella cheese,
   diced

Combine all ingredients in a 5-quart slow cooker; stir well. Cover and cook on low setting for 4 to 5 hours, until hot and cheese is melted. Serves 6.

Hasty Tasty Super-Moist Cornbread

Rheta Merrell
Rutherfordton, NC

I had cooked a huge country meal and at the last minute, I realized I had no bread. This quick & easy recipe sure did come in handy...it was a hit!

1/3 c. butter, sliced
2 eggs, lightly beaten
8-oz. container sour cream
1 c. canned creamed corn

1 c. self-rising white or
   yellow cornmeal
Optional: hot pepper sauce
   to taste

Place butter in a 9" cast-iron skillet. Set in the oven to melt at 400 degrees for 5 minutes. In a bowl, stir together eggs, sour cream and corn. Whisk in cornmeal and hot sauce, if using, just until combined. Carefully pour batter into hot skillet. Bake at 400 degrees for 30 minutes, or until golden. Cut into wedges to serve. Makes 6 to 7 servings.

Canned hominy makes a tasty, filling addition to any southwestern-style soup.

Soups & Breads

Creamy Chicken Chili

Angela Bissette
Middlesex, NC

This recipe is both delicious and easy to prepare. Add a crisp tossed salad and homemade crusty bread for a complete meal.

4 boneless chicken thighs,
   cooked and diced
2 15-oz. cans Great Northern
   beans
10-3/4 oz. can cream of
   chicken soup

32-oz. container chicken broth
10-oz. can diced tomatoes with
   green chiles
Garnish: shredded Cheddar
   cheese, sour cream

In a large soup pot, combine chicken, undrained beans, soup, broth and tomatoes. Bring to a boil over medium-high heat. Reduce heat to medium-low. Simmer, stirring occasionally, for 30 to 45 minutes. Garnish individual servings as desired. Makes 8 servings.

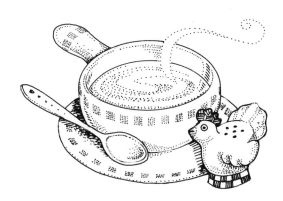

Nothing hits the spot in chilly weather like a bowl of hot soup! Make a double or triple batch of chicken soup, adding only basic veggies and seasonings. Divide into portions and freeze. Noodles or rice can be added when soup is reheated for serving.

German-Style Pork Stew

Annette Ingram
Grand Rapids, MI

This hearty stew is perfect for cool fall weather. Serve with warm buttered rye rolls and warm applesauce.

2 lbs. boneless pork shoulder, trimmed and cubed
16-oz. pkg. refrigerated diced potatoes

2 12-oz. jars mushroom gravy
1-1/2 c. apple juice
2 t. caraway seed

Lightly spray a skillet with cooking spray; add pork. Cook over medium heat until golden, stirring often; drain. Transfer pork to a 4-quart slow cooker; add remaining ingredients. Cover and cook on low setting for 7 to 8 hours. Serves 4.

Smile Soup

Peggy Market
Elida, OH

This scrumptious ham & green bean soup is always requested at work whenever we have a soup carry-in. The flavor is wonderful and it is so very easy to make. The recipe can be doubled and kept warm in a slow cooker for all-day comfort food!

2 10-3/4 oz. cans cream of mushroom soup
1/2 c. milk
2 14-1/2 oz. cans cut green beans, drained

2 c. cooked ham, diced or shredded
pepper to taste

Whisk together soup and milk in a saucepan over medium heat. Stir in beans, ham and pepper. Cook for 5 to 10 minutes, until hot and bubbly. Makes 4 servings.

A quick fix for watery soup... thicken with just a sprinkling of instant potato flakes.

Soups & Breads

Cabbage Beef Soup

Judi Towner
Pinehurst, NC

Even those who say they don't like cabbage love this soup! It's known as Kapousta and is easy to make...very savory and good any time of year. Serve with buttered crusty bread and a green salad.

1 lb. lean ground beef
1 onion, chopped
2 15-oz. cans Italian-style
    stewed tomatoes

15-oz. can diced tomatoes
1 small cabbage, chopped
salt and pepper to taste

Brown beef and onion in a stockpot over medium heat; drain well. Add all tomatoes with juice, cabbage, salt and pepper. Bring to a boil; reduce heat to low and simmer for 35 minutes. Makes 6 to 8 servings.

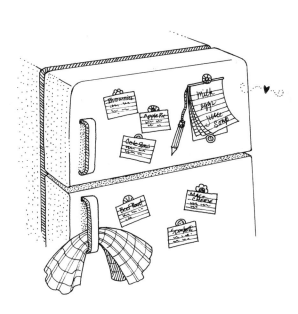

Create mini recipe cards listing the ingredients of tried & true dinner recipes. Glue a button magnet on the back and place on the fridge... so handy whenever it's time to make out a shopping list!

Creamy Chicken & Dumpling Noodle Soup

Sharon Pirkle
Douglasville, GA

Homestyle comfort in a soup pot!

4 boneless, skinless chicken
  breasts
12-oz. pkg. dumpling noodles,
  uncooked

2 12-oz. cans evaporated milk
seasoned salt to taste

Place chicken in a soup pot; cover with water. Simmer over medium heat until tender, about 30 minutes. Cool chicken and dice; reserve 2 to 3 cups chicken broth in pot. Meanwhile, cook noodles according to package directions; drain. Add noodles, chicken, evaporated milk and seasoned salt to reserved broth. Simmer over low heat, stirring occasionally, for about 30 minutes. Serves 6 to 8.

Cozy Chicken Noodle Soup

Amy Thomason Hunt
Traphill, NC

This is my most-requested soup at church in the cold fall and winter months. It's simple to put together.

16-oz. pkg. narrow egg noodles,
  uncooked
4 4-oz. cans chicken
2 14-oz. cans chicken broth
10-3/4 oz. can cream of
  celery soup

10-3/4 oz. can cream of
  chicken soup
salt and pepper to taste
Optional: poultry seasoning
  to taste

Cook noodles according to package directions, but for half the suggested time; drain. Combine noodles, undrained chicken and remaining ingredients in a 4-quart slow cooker. Cover and cook on low setting for 2 to 3 hours. Serves 8 to 10.

Pick a regular theme for each weeknight...dinner planning will be a snap. Some fun themes are Spaghetti Night, Soup & Salad Night and Taco Night. Your family is sure to think of others!

Soups & Breads

American-Style Pho

Carly St. Clair
Lynnwood, WA

On a cold day, I made this soup for my son and myself.
We loved it so much we just had to share it!

3 3-oz. pkgs. chicken-flavored
    ramen noodles, uncooked
6 c. water
12-oz. can chicken

6 green onions, diced
1/3 head cabbage, sliced into
    long thin strips, or 2 to
    3 c. shredded coleslaw mix

In a large saucepan, cook ramen noodles in water according to package instructions. Stir in seasoning packets; do not drain. Add chicken with juices; heat through. To serve, divide onions and cabbage among 6 soup bowls; reserve some of each for garnish. Ladle soup into bowls. Garnish with reserved onions and cabbage. Serves 6.

March 13 is National Chicken Noodle Soup Day. Celebrate by delivering a pot of everybody's favorite soup and a basket of warm rolls to a friend or neighbor. What a welcome surprise on a chilly day!

Chicken-Rice Veggie Soup

Audrey Lett
Newark, DE

This satisfying soup can be stirred up in less than 30 minutes.
We like it with hot buttered rolls on a rainy day.

10-oz. pkg. frozen long-cooking
    white rice in steamer bag
10-oz. pkg. frozen mixed
    vegetables in steamer bag
4 c. chicken broth

2 c. cooked chicken, diced
1/8 t. dried thyme
1/2 t. salt
1/8 t. pepper

Prepare rice and vegetables separately, according to package directions.
Combine rice and vegetables in a large saucepan; add remaining
ingredients. Bring to a boil over high heat. Reduce heat to low and
simmer for 5 to 10 minutes. Makes 6 servings.

Keep some poultry seasoning on hand for savory soups and stews.
Just a shake adds thyme, sage, marjoram, rosemary, nutmeg and
pepper all at once. It's like a spice rack in a jar!

SIMPLE
Soups & Breads

Butter Biscuits

Jess Brunink
Whitehall, MI

This is a recipe that my kids can't get enough of. In fact, my dog ate five of them from my last batch...he got them off the counter when I left the room!

1/2 c. butter, melted
3 c. biscuit baking mix
1 t. sugar

1/8 t. salt
1/3 c. milk or water

Combine all ingredients in a large bowl; mix well. Spray a muffin tin with non-stick vegetable spray. Add dough to muffin cups, one tablespoon per cup. Bake at 375 degrees for 8 to 10 minutes. Makes one dozen.

Tender Spoon Rolls

Claire Bertram
Lexington, KY

Handy for small families! Any unused batter can be kept, covered in the fridge, to bake in the next week.

1 env. active dry yeast
2 c. warm water, 100 to
    110 degrees
4 c. self-rising flour

1/4 c. sugar
3/4 c. butter, melted
1 egg, lightly beaten

Combine yeast and warm water in a large bowl; let stand for 5 minutes. Stir in remaining ingredients until blended. Spoon dough into well-greased muffin cups, filling 2/3 full. Bake at 400 degrees for 20 minutes, or until golden. Makes about one dozen rolls.

It's easy to save leftover fresh herbs. Spoon chopped herbs into an ice cube tray, one tablespoon per cube. Cover with water and freeze. Frozen cubes can be dropped right into hot soup.

31

Bacon-Cheeseburger Soup

Beth Richter
Canby, MN

I started making this soup one winter. I am a fan of slow cooking and wanted something new and different. The first time I made it, I was in love. I made it for our family Christmas and everyone liked it...even the kids were asking for seconds and thirds! Now, everyone asks for my recipe...it's a hit!

1-1/2 lbs. ground beef or turkey,
or a combination
salt and pepper to taste
3-oz. pkg real bacon bits
32-oz. container chicken broth
32-oz. pkg. pasteurized process
cheese, sliced and quartered
24-oz. pkg. frozen southern-
style diced hashbrown
potatoes

Brown meat in a large skillet over medium heat; drain. Season with salt and pepper; transfer to a 6-quart slow cooker. Add remaining ingredients; stir well. Cover and cook on low setting for 6 to 8 hours, until hot and cheese is melted, stirring occasionally. Serves 8 to 12.

Not enough soup bowls on hand for family & friends? Open the cupboards and pull out sturdy mugs! They're just as nice, and the handles make them easy to hold.

Loaded Potato Soup

Tonya Sheppard
Galveston, TX

Since this recipe takes eight hours to cook, it's best to put it on first thing in the morning so it'll be ready when you walk in the door from work.

4 lbs. redskin potatoes, peeled
 and cut into 1/4-inch thick
 slices
1/2 c. onion, chopped
2 14-oz. cans chicken broth
2 t. salt

1/2 t. pepper
2 c. half-and-half
Garnish: shredded Cheddar
 cheese, cooked and
 crumbled bacon, sliced
 green onions

Layer sliced potatoes in a lightly greased 5-quart slow cooker; top with chopped onion. Stir together chicken broth, salt and pepper; pour over potatoes and onion. Broth will not completely cover potatoes and onion. Cover and cook on low setting 8 hours, or until potatoes are tender. Mash mixture with a potato masher; stir in half-and-half. Cover and cook on high setting 20 more minutes, or until mixture is thoroughly heated. Ladle into bowls and garnish. Serves 8.

Minted Spring Pea Soup

Tina Wright
Atlanta, GA

I like to serve this delicate soup topped with a dollop of Greek yogurt and a sprig of fresh mint.

1 c. onion, chopped
2 T. butter
2 c. chicken broth

2 c. frozen baby peas
3/4 c. fresh mint, chopped
salt and pepper to taste

In a large saucepan over medium heat, sauté onion in butter. Add broth; bring to a boil. Add frozen peas; return to a boil. Add mint; stir until mint is wilted. With an immersion blender, puree soup to desired consistency; season with salt and pepper. Serve warm or chilled. Makes 4 servings.

Quick & Spicy Beef Soup

Teri Austin
Jenks, OK

I got this recipe from a friend many years ago and made a few changes to suit our family. It's so good on a really cold day! It's simple to do and easy to keep the ingredients on hand. This is the kind of soup that you can add anything you want to it. I have added potatoes, wide egg noodles and macaroni, all of which are very good. I love to fix a sweet cornbread to go with it.

1/2 to 1 lb. very lean
    ground beef
1 T. dried minced onions
10-oz. can diced tomatoes
    and green chiles
14-oz. can Italian-style green
    beans, drained

10-oz. pkg. frozen mixed
    vegetables, cooked
salt and pepper to taste
1 to 2 c. water
Optional: 2 T. cornstarch

In a soup pot over medium heat, cook beef and onion until browned; drain. Add tomatoes with juice, green beans, mixed vegetables and enough water to cover well. Season with salt and pepper. Bring to a boil. Reduce heat to medium-low and simmer for 20 to 30 minutes, stirring occasionally. For a thicker soup, combine cornstarch with a small amount of water in a small bowl; stir to make a smooth paste. Add cornstarch mixture to soup; bring to a boil again. Cook until soup thickens slightly. Makes 6 to 8 servings.

Make biscuit toppers for bowls of thick, hearty soup...they're almost like mini pot pies. Flatten jumbo refrigerated biscuits and bake according to package directions. Top each soup bowl with a biscuit and dig in!

SIMPLE
Soups & Breads

Daddy's Corned Beef Soup

Bonnie Rogers
Goldshore, NC

My dad made up this soup recipe one night, when he needed to feed a hungry child. It can be made in no time if you need a quick meal.

12-oz. can corned beef,
   broken up
1 onion, diced
14-1/2 oz. can diced tomatoes
14-3/4 oz. can creamed corn

14-1/2 oz. can baby lima beans
salt and pepper to taste
Optional: shredded Cheddar
   cheese

In a large saucepan, combine all ingredients except optional cheese; do not drain tomatoes. Cook over medium heat until heated through and onion is tender. Serve topped with cheese, if desired. Makes 4 to 6 servings.

Take time to share family stories and traditions with your kids over the dinner table. A cherished family recipe can be a super conversation starter.

Easy Sausage-Potato Soup

Laura Flood
Markleville, IN

*The perfect soup when you have a busy evening ahead! Just pop it
in the slow cooker in the morning and go about your day.*

1-1/2 lbs. ground pork sausage
4 potatoes, peeled and cubed
14-1/2 oz. can crushed tomatoes
2 c. water

1 cube beef bouillon
1/8 t. pepper
Garnish: sour cream, shredded
Cheddar cheese

Brown sausage in a skillet over medium heat; drain. Transfer sausage
to a 5-quart slow cooker. Add potatoes, tomatoes with juice, water,
bouillon and pepper; stir well. Cover and cook on low setting for
7 to 8 hours. Serve topped with sour cream and shredded cheese.
Makes 6 servings.

Don't toss the rind from a chunk of Parmesan cheese...there's plenty
of flavor in it! Toss it into your next pot of vegetable soup.
The rind will dissolve, adding rich taste to the soup.

Soups & Breads

Easy Ground Beef Stew

Connie McKone
Fort Atkinson, IA

This is a good and easy slow-cooker stew. My husband loves to take it along when he goes hunting.

2 lbs. ground beef, browned
   and drained
5 potatoes, peeled and diced

2 10-3/4 oz. cans tomato soup
2 10-3/4 oz. cans vegetable
   beef soup

Combine all ingredients in a 5-quart slow cooker; stir. Cover and cook on high setting for 6 hours, or until potatoes are tender. Turn to low setting; cook for 3 to 4 hours. Makes 4 to 6 servings.

French Onion Soup

Joseph Balcer
North Las Vegas, NV

This delicious soup is usually ordered at restaurants, but it's just as easy to make at home.

5 T. butter, divided
2 c. onions, sliced
6 c. beef broth
1/8 t. salt

1/8 t. pepper
4 slices French bread
grated Parmesan cheese to taste

Melt 4 tablespoons butter in a soup pot. Sauté onions over medium heat until deep golden brown, about 45 minutes. Add broth and simmer for 30 to 40 minutes. Shortly before serving, toast bread slices under the broiler until golden on both sides. Sprinkle one side with grated cheese; dot with remaining butter. Broil until bubbly. Ladle soup into soup bowls; float toasts in soup. Serves 4.

Twisty bread sticks are a tasty go-with for soup. Brush refrigerated bread sticks with a little beaten egg and dust with garlic powder, then pop in the oven until toasty.

Chili-Weather Chili

Mary Jo Babiarz
Spring Grove, IL

Serve with Italian bread and a plate of fresh fruit
for a complete meal.

1 lb. ground beef
2 T. onion, diced
15-3/4 oz. can chili beans with
   chili sauce

16-oz. can tomato sauce
8-oz. jar salsa
Garnish: shredded cheese

Brown beef and onion together in a large stockpot; drain. Add remaining ingredients except garnish. Bring to a boil and reduce heat to medium; add 1/2 cup water if mixture is too thick. Cover and simmer for 30 minutes, stirring occasionally. Garnish with shredded cheese. Serves 4.

Cheddar Corn Muffins

Lisa Langston
Conroe, TX

Just a good ol' muffin to eat with about anything!
Delicious hot from the oven.

8-1/2 oz. pkg. corn muffin mix
1/2 c. milk
2 c. corn

1/4 c. onion, finely chopped
1 c. shredded Cheddar cheese

In a large bowl, prepare mix with milk according to box directions. Stir in corn, cheese and onion. Spoon batter into greased muffin cups, filling 1/2 full. Bake at 350 degrees until lightly golden, about 25 to 30 minutes. Let cool slightly before serving. Makes one dozen.

Spoon leftover soup into muffin cups and freeze, then store
the cubes in a plastic freezer bag...ready to reheat for a quick lunch.

SIMPLE
Soups & Breads

Carnitas Soup

Donna Landwehr
Wheat Ridge, CO

This soup was made in a pinch for dinner one night, using items on hand. It's a very warming and hearty soup. It's also easy to double or triple the recipe and freeze the extra. The heat level can easily be changed up by mixing mild and spicy tomatoes.

2 10-oz. cans diced tomatoes
    and green chiles
15-oz. can black beans, drained
    and rinsed

2 14-oz. cans chicken broth
16-oz. pkg. pre-cooked pork
    carnitas, diced

Combine all ingredients in a soup pot over medium heat, adding desired amount of carnitas. Amount of broth may be adjusted to desired consistency. Cook until heated through, stirring occasionally, about 30 minutes. Serves 4.

Grilled bread is perfect with hot soup. Brush thick slices of French bread with olive oil and add a shake of coarse salt and pepper. Grill or broil on both sides until toasted and golden.

Chili Dog Soup

Katie Marberry
Valley, AL

I created this recipe while in college, and it has now become a staple on my family's table. Customize this recipe by adding your family's personal favorite chili dog toppings. Kids love it! Serve with toasted hot dog buns or white bread.

15-oz. can chili
3 hot dogs, cut into thin rounds
3/4 c. pasteurized process
　　cheese sauce

2 T. mustard
2 to 3 T. onion, diced

Combine chili, hot dogs and cheese sauce in a saucepan; simmer over medium heat for 10 minutes. Stir in mustard and onion. Continue cooking until hot dogs are heated through and soup is beginning to boil. Serves 3.

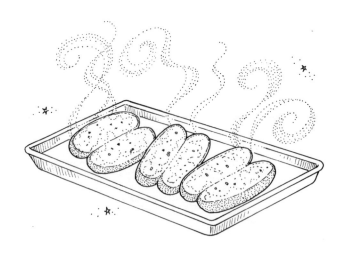

Turn leftover hot dog buns into garlic bread sticks in a jiffy.
Spread buns with softened butter, sprinkle with garlic
salt and broil until toasty.

SIMPLE
Soups & Breads

Vonna's Soup

Fran Ryan
Los Lunas, NM

*This soup is named after my sister-in-law who gave me the recipe.
So easy and so tasty! Great served with bread sticks, garlic bread
or buttered French bread.*

1 lb. ground beef
10-3/4 oz. can tomato soup
10-3/4 oz. can bean with
    bacon soup

15-oz. can mixed vegetables,
    drained
2-1/2 c. water
taco seasoning mix to taste

Brown beef in a soup pot over medium heat; drain. Add soups,
vegetables and water. Bring to a boil. Reduce heat to low; simmer for
10 minutes. Stir in taco seasoning to taste; simmer for 5 more minutes.
Serves 4 to 6.

Easy Cheesy Veggie Soup

Sara Huntley
Dodge Center, MN

*This is a very quick & easy soup to make...perfect for our
cold Minnesota winters!*

3 14-1/2 oz. cans fat-free
    chicken broth
2 16-oz. pkgs. frozen
    cauliflower, broccoli and
    carrot mix

10-oz. can diced tomatoes with
    green chiles
10-oz. pkg. light pasteurized
    process cheese, cubed

Bring broth to a boil in a soup pot over high heat. Add frozen
vegetables; cook until tender. Reduce heat to medium-low; stir in
tomatoes with juice and cheese. Cook, stirring often, until cheese is
melted. Makes 10 servings.

Sometimes a bowl of hot chicken noodle soup is just what you need...
right now! Cook up a package of chicken-flavored ramen noodles
and stir in a small can of chicken with a little parsley.
You'll be feeling better in a jiffy.

Easy Cheesy Broccoli Soup

Bethi Hendrickson
Danville, PA

This is a wonderful quick recipe. Serve it with a crunchy salad and supper is complete.

14-oz. pkg. frozen broccoli
   flowerets
2 10-3/4 oz. cans Cheddar
   cheese soup

2 c. milk
1 T. all-purpose flour
2 c. shredded Cheddar cheese,
   divided

Place broccoli in a microwave-safe casserole dish. Microwave on high for 5 minutes. Meanwhile, whisk together soup, milk and flour in a soup pot. Stir until smooth; cook over medium-low heat until warmed through. Drain cooked broccoli; add to soup mixture. Cook for 10 minutes over medium heat, stirring frequently. Add cheese, reserving 1/4 cup for garnish. Cook over low heat for an additional 3 minutes. Ladle into soup bowls and top with a sprinkle of reserved cheese. Makes 8 servings.

Try substituting canned evaporated milk for half-and-half or whole milk. It's handy to keep in the pantry, doesn't need refrigeration and is lower in fat too.

Soups & Breads

Tomato-Macaroni Soup

Terri Scungio
Williamsburg, VA

This was one of my husband's favorite dishes from his childhood. Plain tomato soup with cooked macaroni added...so simple! I have added a few ingredients and it is loved by both kids and adults. This can be made ahead and kept warm in a slow cooker for large crowds.

1-1/4 c. elbow macaroni, uncooked
2 10-3/4 oz. cans tomato soup
2-1/2 c. evaporated or whole milk

Optional: 1/2 t. salt
1/4 t. pepper
1-1/2 t. Italian seasoning

Cook macaroni according to package directions; drain. Meanwhile, in a saucepan, whisk together soup and milk; add seasonings. Cook over medium-high heat, stirring often, until warm. Stir in cooked macaroni and continue cooking until heated through. Makes 6 to 8 servings.

Sprightly Bread

Kristin Stone
Little Elm, TX

I love, love, love beer bread. But, I don't love beer. I finally came up with a solution...why not use lemon-lime soda? This quick bread is a perfect accompaniment to soups. We love to eat it in the fall!

2-1/2 c. self-rising flour
3 T. sugar
1 egg, beaten

12-oz. can lemon-lime soda
1 T. butter, melted

Combine flour, sugar, egg and soda in a bowl. Stir well and pour into a greased 9"x5" loaf pan. Drizzle melted butter over batter. Bake at 350 degrees for about 45 minutes, until top is cracked and golden. Makes one loaf.

To mellow the flavor of tomato soup, stir in a teaspoon of sugar.

Easy Breezy Potato Soup

Sandy Coffey
Cincinnati, OH

This is an easy soup to fix on the spur of the moment

3/4 c. water
1-1/2 c. potatoes, peeled
   and cubed
1 T. butter
1 T. onion, chopped

3/4 t. salt
2 c. milk, divided
2-1/2 T. all-purpose flour
Optional: shredded cheese,
   bacon bits

Bring water to a boil in a saucepan over high heat. Add potatoes, butter, onion and salt. Cook until potatoes are tender; do not drain. Stir in 1-1/2 cups milk; heat through. Whisk together remaining milk and flour in a cup; stir into soup. Cook for one to 2 minutes longer, until thickened. Garnish as desired. Serves 2.

Family & Friends Chicken Soup

Kayla Herring
Hartwell, GA

My family & friends request this soup when they aren't feeling well.
It's an easy soup to toss together on a cold winter night.

2 10-3/4 oz. cans cream of
   chicken soup
2 32-oz. containers chicken
   broth
2 13-oz. cans chicken, flaked

salt and pepper to taste
8-oz. pkg. thin egg noodles,
   or 2 boil-in bags instant
   rice, cooked

Combine all ingredients except rice or noodles. Simmer until heated through. Stir in desired amount of cooked rice or noodles and serve. Serves 6 to 8.

Worries go down better
with soup than without.
– Jewish Proverb

TASTY
Salads & Sides

Summer Garden Salad

Ramona Wysong
Barlow, KY

A taste I've grown up with! This salad was a part of our meals for as long as I remember, all summer long. I added the cucumber as I got older, and I've taken it to work for lunch many, many times. The simplest, freshest ingredients, basic seasonings, no dressings, so the fresh taste of the vegetables can really shine. Served chilled, it's so refreshing on those long hot summer days.

3 ripe tomatoes, chopped
1 green, red, orange or yellow
   pepper, chopped
1 cucumber, peeled, seeded
   and chopped

1 sweet onion, chopped
salt and pepper to taste
Optional: lemon pepper or
   Creole seasoning to taste

Combine all vegetables in a serving bowl. Season with salt, pepper and your favorite seasoning blend. Cover and refrigerate several hours before serving. Makes 4 servings.

Kids are more likely to eat their salad if vegetables are cut into bite-size pieces that are easily eaten with a fork or spoon. A mix of crunchy textures (never soggy!) and bright colors is sure to appeal to young appetites.

Tomato & Feta Salad

Janae Mallonee
Marlboro, MA

This is something we ate a lot of, growing up. It is just the perfect summer salad. My hubby asks me to make this whenever we have steak. He likes a little diced red onion with his, so I put it on the side for him. When there is extra salad left over, save it to enjoy the next day for lunch with a chunk of Italian bread...heaven!

1 pt. cherry or grape tomatoes,
   cut into half or thirds
1/2 c. crumbled feta cheese

1/4 c. Italian salad dressing
Optional: diced red onion
   to taste

In a serving bowl, mix all ingredients. Serve immediately. Makes 4 servings.

Cottage Cheese Salad

Robin Cox
Collinsville, OK

A delicious summer side that's always requested for barbecues.

24-oz. container cottage cheese
1 bunch green onions, diced
1 cucumber, diced

2 ripe tomatoes, diced
1 green pepper, diced
salt and pepper to taste

Spoon cottage cheese into a serving bowl. Add vegetables and stir gently; season with salt and pepper. Cover and refrigerate until serving time. Make 8 servings.

Going to the farmers' market? Bring along an ice chest and several ice packs if you won't be returning home right away. Perishable produce will stay fresh and crisp.

Green Bean & Blue Cheese Salad

Irene Robinson
Cincinnati, OH

Try this unique salad...you'll love it! Easy to double.

1-1/2 c. fresh green beans,
  snapped
1/2 c. whole black olives, halved
  lengthwise

1/2 c. crumbled blue cheese
2 T. olive oil
1/4 t. salt
1/8 t. pepper

Cover green beans with water in a small saucepan. Bring to a boil over medium-high heat. Cook, uncovered, for 8 to 10 minutes, until crisp. Drain; transfer beans to a bowl. Cover and refrigerate. Add remaining ingredients; chill until serving time. Makes 2 servings.

Cauliflower Summer Salad

Gladys Kielar
Whitehouse, OH

An easy make-ahead salad everyone will love.

1 head cauliflower, cut into
  bite-size flowerets
10-oz. pkg. frozen peas
1 c. Cheddar cheese, diced

1-oz. pkg. ranch salad
  dressing mix
1-1/2 c. mayonnaise

In a serving bowl, combine cauliflower, frozen peas, cheese and salad dressing mix; toss well. Spread mayonnaise over the top, sealing to the edges. Cover and refrigerate overnight. Stir gently just before serving. Serves 6.

Keep a crock of herbed garlic butter in the fridge for seasoning steamed veggies or making garlic bread. Blend a teaspoon each of Italian seasoning, dried mustard and garlic powder into 1/2 cup softened butter. Mmm good!

Spinach-Feta Melon Salad

Terry Davis
The Villages, FL

I love to relax with a tasty salad after working out in the pool...
something light and refreshing like this one!

2 c. fresh spinach leaves
1 c. watermelon cubes
1/2 peach, pitted and chopped

2 T. crumbled feta cheese
2 T. Catalina salad dressing

Divide spinach leaves between 2 salad plates. Top with watermelon, peach and feta cheese. Drizzle with salad dressing; serve immediately. Makes 2 servings.

Turn a tossed salad into a lunchtime jar salad. To a wide-mouth Mason jar, add desired salad dressing, then layer with firm ingredients like cucumber, melon and beans. Add soft or crumbly ingredients like fresh greens, chopped egg and cheese crumbles; close jar. At lunchtime, invert the jar and shake to mix in the dressing. Grab a fork and enjoy your salad!

Crunchy Corn Salad

Elizabeth Smithson
Cunningham, KY

*My friend Mary brought this to a monthly homemakers' dinner.
I loved it and got the recipe from her...now I make it
often. My grandchildren love it too!*

2 15-1/4 oz. cans corn, drained
2 c. shredded Cheddar cheese
1 c. mayonnaise-style salad
  dressing
1 green pepper, chopped

2 T. canned chopped jalapeño
  peppers
Garnish: 8-1/2 oz. pkg. barbecue
  corn chips, divided

Mix all ingredients except corn chips in a serving bowl. Cover and chill
if not serving immediately. Just before serving, crush 1/2 bag of chips,
or more as desired; sprinkle over salad. Reserve remaining chips for
another use. Makes 10 servings.

Pea Perfect Salad

Teresa Eller
Kansas City, KS

*You'll love this yummy salad! Sometimes I'll use mixed veggies
instead of the peas...it's a nice change.*

10-oz. pkg. frozen peas
2 eggs, hard-boiled, peeled
  and diced

1/4 onion, finely chopped
1/2 c. Colby Jack cheese, diced
1 c. mayonnaise

Cook peas according to package directions; drain and cool. Combine
peas, eggs, onion and cheese in a bowl. Add mayonnaise; stir to blend.
Serve immediately, or cover and chill. Serves 4 to 6.

Popcorn croutons! Use up leftover
party popcorn the next day by tossing
it with olive oil, garlic powder and
Italian seasoning. Sprinkle on top
of a lunchtime salad.

TASTY
Salads & Sides

Beans, Cheese & Chiles

Jackie Smulski
Lyons, IL

*This casserole adds a lot of flavor to plain refried beans.
Add a little salsa or guacamole for even more zip.*

16-oz. can refried beans
4-oz. can chopped mild green
   chiles
dried cilantro to taste

salt and pepper to taste
1-1/2 c. shredded Mexican-
   blend or sharp Cheddar
   cheese, divided

In a large microwave-safe bowl, combine beans, chiles, seasonings
and one cup cheese. Microwave on high for about 30 to 40 seconds;
mix well. Transfer to a greased 8"x8" baking pan and spread evenly.
Top with remaining cheese. Bake, uncovered, at 325 degrees for
20 to 25 minutes, until cheese is melted. Makes 4 servings.

Chili Relleno Casserole

Michelle Powell
Valley, AL

This makes a great easy side dish on a Mexican buffet or taco night!

27-oz. can green chile pepper
   strips, drained and divided
32-oz. pkg. shredded Cheddar
   Jack cheese, divided

4 eggs, beaten
1 c. milk
3 T. biscuit baking mix

In a greased 13"x9" baking pan, layer half each of chiles and cheese;
repeat layers and set aside. In a bowl, whisk eggs with milk. Stir in
baking mix and pour over top. Bake, uncovered, at 350 degrees for
40 minutes, until bubbly and golden. Makes 8 servings.

Shake up a tasty dressing for lettuce,
tomato and avocado salad. In a jar, combine
3 tablespoons olive oil, 2 tablespoons lime
juice, 1/4 teaspoon dry mustard and
1/2 teaspoon salt. Cover and shake
until well blended.

Cheesy Hominy

Patti Wafford
Mount Vernon, TX

My family always requests this as a side when we're having
my mom's homemade hot tamales. It's ooey-gooey goodness
and is so simple to make!

2 15-1/2 oz. cans yellow
hominy, drained
10-3/4 oz. can cream of
celery soup

8-oz. pkg. Mexican or regular
pasteurized process cheese,
cubed

Combine hominy, soup and cheese in a microwave-safe dish.
Microwave on high until cheese is melted, stirring every few minutes.
Makes 6 to 8 servings.

Zesty Black-Eyed Peas

Angela Bissette
Middlesex, NJ

This simple recipe is excellent served with pork and also
can be served over rice. For a less spicy version, just substitute
an undrained can of stewed tomatoes for the tomatoes with chiles.

1/2 c. onion, diced
2 T. garlic, minced
1 T. oil

2 15-oz cans black-eyed peas
10-oz. can diced tomatoes with
green chiles

In a skillet over medium heat, sauté onion and garlic in oil for
5 minutes. Stir in undrained peas and tomatoes. Reduce heat to low;
simmer for 15 to 20 minutes. Serves 6.

Instead of bread, serve warm flour tortillas with your favorite
Mexican dish. Place several tortillas on a microwave-safe plate
and cover with a dampened paper towel. Microwave on high
for 30 seconds to one minute.

Salads & Sides

Sidekick Veggies

Charlene McCain
Bakersfield, CA

This is the perfect side dish for any dinner or barbecue. It also works very well as the filling for a chicken pot pie. It's best served hot.

6 red potatoes, diced	3 stalks celery, chopped
3 carrots, peeled and sliced	4 T. butter, cubed
1 onion, diced	salt and pepper to taste

Combine vegetables in a microwave-safe dish. Add enough water to nearly cover vegetables; cover with a lid. Microwave on high for 25 minutes, or until vegetables are fork-tender. Drain; transfer vegetables to an ungreased 13"x9" baking pan. Lightly sprinkle with salt and pepper; dot with butter. Place pan under the broiler for about 10 minutes, until potatoes begin to turn golden, being careful not to burn. Stir just before serving; add more salt and pepper as desired. Makes 6 to 8 servings.

Grill up a salad! Choose small heads of romaine, and don't separate the leaves. Spritz with olive oil and grill over high heat for 2 to 3 minutes per side, until lightly wilted and golden. Serve lettuce drizzled with balsamic vinaigrette, or chop and use in a Caesar salad.

Chelsea's Cheesy Potatoes

Chelsea Groves
Chillicothe, OH

This is my go-to for any dinner or get-together whenever a covered dish is needed. Everybody loves it!

10-3/4 oz. can cream of
  mushroom soup
10-3/4 oz. can cream of
  chicken soup
1 T. plus 1 t. sour cream

32-oz. pkg. frozen diced
  hashbrowns, thawed
1 to 2 16-oz. pkgs. shredded
  Cheddar cheese

Stir together soups and sour cream in a saucepan over medium heat until warm. Spread hashbrowns in a lightly greased 13"x9" baking pan. Spoon soup mixture over top; stir gently until hashbrowns are covered. Top with desired amount of cheese. Bake, uncovered, at 350 degrees for 30 to 40 minutes. Serves 4 to 6.

Pam's Nacho Cheese Potatoes

Pam Peterson
Crystal, ND

I was getting tired of the same old potato casseroles until I tried this recipe...mmm!

5 potatoes, peeled and sliced
2 onions, sliced
1 to 2 c. cooked ham, diced
8-oz. container whipping cream

2 10-3/4 oz. cans nacho
  cheese soup
salt and pepper to taste

Combine all ingredients in a large bowl; toss gently to mix. Transfer to a 13"x9" baking pan sprayed with non-stick vegetable spray. Bake, uncovered, at 350 degrees for about 2 hours. Makes 8 servings.

Out of bottled salad dressing? It takes only a few minutes to mix up your own! Combine 3/4 cup canola oil with 1/4 cup white wine vinegar; add salt and pepper to taste. Shake well and let sit a few minutes so the flavors can blend.

Fiesta Corn Casserole

Mary Jefferson Rabon
Mobile, AL

*I was given this recipe 20 years ago. It is a favorite side dish
for Thanksgiving and Christmas for my family!*

5-oz. pkg. long-cooking yellow
  rice, uncooked
1/4 c. butter, melted
2 11-oz. cans sweet corn and
  diced peppers

10-3/4 oz. can cream of celery
  soup
8-oz. pkg. shredded sharp
  Cheddar cheese, divided

Cook rice according to package directions; stir in butter, corn and soup.
Stir in one cup of cheese, or more as desired. Transfer to a lightly
greased 13"x9" baking pan. Bake, uncovered, at 325 degrees for
25 minutes, or until bubbly and cheese is melted. Top with remaining
cheese and bake for 5 more minutes. Serves 8 to 10.

Casseroles spell comfort food, but what if the recipe is large and
your family is small? Simple...just divide the ingredients into
2 small dishes and freeze one for later!

Mom's Baked Butter Beans

Ardice Holbrook
Manchester, MD

*My mom has made these beans for every holiday and
every time, they are a big hit.*

2 16-oz. cans butter beans
28-oz. can diced tomatoes
1 onion, chopped
1 c. brown sugar, packed

2 to 3 slices bacon, cut into
   1-inch pieces
2 t. salt

Pour undrained beans into a lightly greased 13"x9" baking pan. Add
tomatoes with juice and remaining ingredients; stir until well mixed
together. Bake, uncovered, at 350 degrees for 2 hours, or until hot,
bubbly and bacon is cooked. Makes 8 servings.

This is my invariable advice to people:
Learn how to cook...try new recipes,
learn from your mistakes, be fearless,
and above all, have fun!
– Julia Child

TASTY
Salads & Sides

Rosetta's Easy Potato Salad

Pearl Teiserskas
Brookfield, IL

My grandmother used to make this simple recipe for the family when we lived in Key West, Florida. It is simple yet oh-so good.

5 lbs. white potatoes, peeled
   and cubed
30-oz. jar mayonnaise
1 doz. eggs, hard-cooked, peeled
   and chopped

4 stalks celery, diced
2 T. mustard-style hot dog
   relish

Cover potatoes with water in a large saucepan. Cook over high heat until fork-tender, about 20 minutes. Drain potatoes; transfer to a large serving bowl. When cool, add remaining ingredients; stir gently until well mixed. Cover and chill until serving time. Makes 12 servings.

Hot Bacon-Potato Salad

Amber Erskine
Hartland, VT

This salad is just right for toting to a family reunion.

1/4 lb. bacon
3/4 c. celery, sliced
1/2 c. onion, chopped
1-1/2 T. all-purpose flour
3/4 c. water
1/3 c. vinegar

2 T. sugar
1-1/2 t. salt
1 t. mustard
1/4 t. celery seed
4 c. potatoes, peeled,
   cooked and sliced

Cook bacon in a skillet over medium heat until crisp. Remove bacon; crumble and set aside. Add celery and onion to drippings in skillet; cook until tender. Add remaining ingredients except potatoes; cook until thickened, stirring constantly. Fold in potatoes and bacon; heat through. Serve warm. Makes 4 to 6 servings.

How to know whether to start fresh vegetables cooking in hot or cold water? Old kitchen wisdom says to start vegetables that grow above the ground in boiling water...below the ground, in cold water.

Cincinnati Salad

Irene Robinson
Cincinnati, OH

The Spanish peanuts stay crisp...they're the secret ingredient! Serve on lettuce for individual servings, or in a bowl for self-service.

1/4 c. sour cream
1/4 c. mayonnaise
2 10-oz. pkgs. frozen peas,
    thawed and drained

1 to 2 green onions, thinly sliced
1/2 lb. redskin Spanish peanuts

Blend sour cream and mayonnaise in a large bowl. Fold in peas and onions; cover and chill. Stir in peanuts just before serving. Makes 8 servings.

Crispy, Nutty, Cheesy Salad

Sharon Lundberg
Longwood, FL

Whenever I serve this salad to family & friends, I receive compliments...and it is so easy to put together.

1/3 c. chopped walnuts
4 to 5 c. fresh spinach
1/3 c. crumbled blue cheese
2 Honey Crisp apples, cored
    and diced

raspberry vinaigrette salad
    dressing to taste

Spread walnuts on an ungreased baking sheet. Bake at 325 degrees for 8 to 10 minutes, until toasted and crunchy; cool. Combine spinach and apples in a serving bowl. Sprinkle with blue cheese and walnuts; toss to mix. Serve with salad dressing. Makes 4 servings.

For a fun after-school snack that's ready in a jiffy, stuff a hollowed-out apple with peanut butter and raisins.

TASTY
Salads & Sides

Dilly Cucumber Salad

Debra Holme
Victoria, Australia

When I moved to Australia, I brought along my Gooseberry Patch books. I absolutely love your books. I've even introduced some of my new Aussie neighbors to them.

4 c. cucumbers, peeled and
    thinly sliced
3/4 c. sour cream
1 T. oil
1 t. sugar

1/2 t. garlic salt
1/2 t. salt
1/2 t. white vinegar
1/4 t. dill weed

Place cucumbers in a serving bowl. Mix next 6 ingredients in a separate bowl; add to cucumbers and toss to coat. Sprinkle dill weed over salad. Cover and refrigerate for at least one hour. Mix lightly before serving. Serves 5 to 6.

Sour Cream Cucumbers

Susi Dickinson
Prentice, WI

This salad is so refreshing. I make it often in the summer, when fresh cucumbers are just a few steps away! If time is very short, I skip chilling the cucumbers in water...it is still good!

3 cucumbers, peeled and thinly
    sliced
2 t. salt, divided
1 sweet onion, thinly sliced and
    separated into rings

1/2 c. sour cream
2 T. cider vinegar
1 t. sugar
1/2 t. pepper

Layer cucumbers in a bowl. Cover with water; add 1-1/2 teaspoons salt. Cover and chill. Drain and rinse cucumbers in fresh water; return to bowl. Add onion rings; toss to mix. In a small bowl, blend sour cream, vinegar and sugar; fold into cucumbers. Season with pepper and remaining salt. Makes 8 servings.

Light Chicken Tortellini Caesar Salad

Pamela Simons
Powell, OH

I created this salad when my kids were little, so I could pull out the chicken for picky eaters and serve it with cut-up fruit for them. My husband and I had a great salad, and our kids got a healthy quick-prep meal. We use the breasts of a rotisserie chicken as a time-saver. The two leftover chicken legs make a great lunch for kids the next day too!

9-oz. pkg. cheese tortellini,
    uncooked and divided
16-oz. bottle light Caesar salad
    dressing, divided
1 deli rotisserie chicken, breasts
    only, shredded or cut into
    chunks

1 head romaine lettuce, chopped
shredded Parmesan cheese
    to taste

Cook half of tortellini according to package directions; drain and rinse with cold water. Save remaining tortellini for another use. Transfer cooked tortellini to a bowl. Add enough salad dressing to coat; mix gently. May be covered and chilled ahead of time. At serving time, combine tortellini, chicken and lettuce. Add more salad dressing to taste; top with a little Parmesan cheese. Makes 6 servings.

Invite friends over for a salad supper on a day that's too hot to cook.
Ask everyone to bring along a favorite salad. You provide crunchy
bread sticks or a basket of muffins and a pitcher of iced tea...enjoy!

Grandma's Shrimp Potato Salad

Julie Hutson
Callahan, FL

This delicate salad always reminds me of warm, summer Saturday afternoons at my grandparents' home. My grandma cooked every day. She always made a big breakfast and then cooked the traditional Southern dinner to be served mid-afternoon. This special salad always takes me right back to her kitchen table...sweet and delicious memories!

6 potatoes, peeled and diced
salt to taste
1 lb. shrimp, boiled, peeled
   and chopped

1 stalk celery, finely chopped
1/2 c. mayonnaise
Optional: crumbled bacon

Cover potatoes with salted water in a large saucepan. Cook over high heat until fork-tender, about 20 minutes; drain. Very lightly mash some of the potatoes. Add remaining ingredients and stir to blend; season with more salt, as desired. Top with crumbled bacon, if desired. Serves 4 to 6.

Hollowed-out peppers can be fun salad bowls! Whether it's a crisp green salad or more of a meal made from chicken, tuna or egg salad, they're just the right size and add a splash of color to the table.

Cheesy Potato, Mushroom & Onion   *Janae Mallonee*
Marlborough, MA

My daughter and I both love melty cheese as a favorite comfort food. I'll ask her what she wants for dinner, and many times the answer is "melted cheese." Sometimes it's grilled cheese, sometimes it's mac & cheese...but most often it's this combo. It's warming, comforting, and (best of all) easy!

3 potatoes, peeled and diced
1/2 onion, diced
8-oz. pkg. sliced mushrooms

1/4 c. pasteurized process
    cheese, diced
salt and pepper to taste

Cover potatoes and onion with water in a large saucepan. Cook over high heat until fork-tender, about 15 minutes; drain. Add mushrooms and cheese; cook and stir until cheese is melted. Add salt and pepper to taste. Makes 6 servings.

It's really a personal preference...choose white, yellow or red onions for anything from salads to cooked dishes. Sweet onions are best raw, or just very lightly cooked to keep their sweet, mild flavor.

Mushroom-Mozzarella Bake

Dana Rowan
Spokane, WA

Sautéed mushrooms in butter, cream and herbs, topped with mozzarella cheese and baked until melty...what's not to love about that? Serve by itself or spooned over a grilled steak. So delicious!

1 lb. sliced mushrooms
3 T. butter
1/2 t. seasoning salt
2 T. whipping cream

1 t. dried parsley
1/4 t. pepper
3/4 to 1 c. shredded mozzarella
   cheese

In a skillet over medium heat, sauté mushrooms in butter until softened. Keep cooking until most of the liquid evaporates. Add seasoning salt; continue to sauté until mushrooms are golden. Reduce heat to low; stir in cream, parsley and pepper. Simmer until cream is slightly reduced. Transfer mushroom mixture to an ungreased shallow 2-quart casserole dish. Sprinkle with cheese. Bake, uncovered, at 350 degrees for 10 minutes, or until cheese is melted. Serves 4 to 6.

Golden Parmesan Roasted Potatoes

Linda Hendrix
Moundville, MO

Pop into the oven alongside a roast for a homestyle dinner that can't be beat.

1/4 c. all-purpose flour
1/4 c. grated Parmesan cheese
3/4 t. salt
1/8 t. pepper

6 potatoes, peeled and cut into
   wedges
1/3 c. butter, melted
Garnish: fresh parsley, chopped

Place flour, cheese, salt and pepper in a large plastic zipping bag; mix well. Add potato wedges; shake to coat. Pour butter into a 13"x9" baking pan, tilting to coat; arrange potatoes in pan. Bake, uncovered, at 375 degrees for one hour. Sprinkle with parsley. Serves 4 to 6.

Save the water that vegetables have been cooked in...it makes a flavorful addition to your next pot of soup.

Pizza Rice

Janis Parr
Ontario, Canada

This is a delicious and fun side dish...one that's popular with young and old alike. It's a nice change from potatoes and French fries. I make it often and we never get tired of it. Be sure to use pizza sauce rather than spaghetti sauce for a real pizza flavor.

2 c. long-cooking rice, uncooked
3 c. pizza sauce
2 c. water
1 c. mushrooms, chopped
2/3 c. pepperoni, cut into bite-size pieces
1 c. shredded mozzarella cheese

In a 4-quart slow cooker, combine uncooked rice and remaining ingredients except cheese. Stir well. Cover and cook on low setting for 10 hours, or on high setting for 6 hours. About 10 minutes before serving, sprinkle cheese on top; cover and let stand until melted. Makes 6 servings.

Mom's Rice Casserole

Sally Lambert
Kokomo, IN

My mom has made this for at least 40 years and has shared it with many. I have added a few of my own touches to suit myself! So easy to make and so pleasing to everyone. This recipe doubles very easily. Great with steak on the grill!

1 c. long-cooking white rice, uncooked
10-1/2 oz. can can French onion soup
10-1/2 oz. can beef consommé
1 to 2 4-oz. cans sliced mushrooms, drained
1/4 to 1/2 c. butter, sliced
Optional: sliced green onions and/or green pepper

Add uncooked rice to a lightly greased 13"x9" baking pan. Pour soups over rice; top with mushrooms and dot evenly with butter. Bake, covered, at 350 degrees for about 1-1/2 hours, until rice is tender and liquid is absorbed. Serves 10 to 12.

Grandma's Romanian Mamaliga cu Branza

Patricia Nau
River Grove, IL

My grandmother made this cornmeal casserole often, especially during Lent. Pronounced "mamaleega," it's delicious! It's similar to Italian polenta. For the authentic flavor, use brick cheese.

4 c. water
1 T. kosher salt
1 c. yellow cornmeal, divided

1/4 c. butter, diced
2 c. brick or Muenster cheese,
   grated and divided

In a saucepan over high heat, bring water and salt to a rolling boil. Sprinkle 1/2 cup of cornmeal over water, stirring constantly with a wooden spoon. Reduce heat to medium-low to avoid spattering. Add remaining cornmeal; cook and stir until thickened. Remove from heat; stir until smooth. Spread half of mixture into a buttered 2-quart casserole dish. Dot with butter. Sprinkle one cup of cheese over the top. Repeat layers, ending with cheese on top. Bake, uncovered, at 350 degrees for 10 to 15 minutes, until bubbly and cheese is melted. Makes 4 to 6 servings.

For hearty salads in a snap, keep unopened cans of diced tomatoes, olives, garbanzo beans and marinated artichokes in the fridge. They'll be chilled and ready to toss with fresh greens or cooked pasta at a moment's notice.

Creamy Italian Noodles

Joan White
Malvern, PA

*Add some leftover cooked chicken or ham to this
side dish and turn it into a main.*

8-oz. pkg. bowtie pasta or wide
   egg noodles, uncooked
1/4 c. butter, softened
1/4 c. grated Parmesan cheese

1/2 c. whipping cream or
   half-and-half
2-1/4 t. Italian salad dressing
   mix

Cook pasta or noodles according to package directions; drain. Transfer
pasta to a large bowl; toss with butter. Add remaining ingredients and
mix well. Serve immediately. Makes 6 servings.

Pasta à la Creamy Pesto

Wendy Ball
Battle Creek, MI

*Thank goodness for ready-to-use products like pesto! They come in
handy on busy days when you don't have a lot of time. Buy a
rotisserie chicken and make this quick side dish...dinner is served!*

16-oz. pkg. penne rigate pasta,
   uncooked
8-oz. pkg. Neufchatel cheese,
   softened, cubed

2 T. butter
6-oz. jar basil pesto or
   sun-dried tomato pesto

Cook pasta according to package directions. Drain, reserving 3/4 cup of
the pasta water. Return pasta back to the pan. Add butter and cheese;
stir until melted. Gently stir in pesto, adding one to 2 tablespoons of
reserved pasta water at a time, to the desired consistency. Makes 4 to
6 servings.

Prevent messy pasta boil-overs! Rub a little vegetable oil
over the top few inches inside the cooking pot.

Salads & Sides

Alex's Noodle Special

Rhonda Gist
Yukon, OK

One day I was babysitting my nephews and ran out of mac & cheese. I had noodles, cheese and tomato sauce on hand, and this was the result. My nephews loved it and thought it was the greatest in the world. They ask for it every time they come over.

12-oz. pkg. dumpling egg
    noodles, uncooked
1 to 2 8-oz. cans tomato sauce

8-oz. pkg. favorite shredded
    cheese

Cook noodles according to package directions; drain and return to the pan. Add tomato sauce to taste; add cheese and stir until cheese is melted. Serve immediately. Makes 8 servings.

Fresh Tomato Pasta

Sara Moulder
LaGrange, OH

Simple and tasty on a hot summer day...a delicious side or meatless main. Add as many tomatoes from your garden as you like.

8-oz. pkg. thin spaghetti,
    uncooked
1/2 c. Italian salad dressing

1/4 c. grated Parmesan cheese
4 ripe tomatoes, cubed
salt and pepper to taste

Cook spaghetti according to package directions; drain. Transfer pasta to a serving bowl; add remaining ingredients and stir gently to coat. Serve immediately while still very warm. Makes 4 servings.

When garden tomatoes aren't in
season, try roma tomatoes...
they're available year 'round and
work well in cooked dishes.

Mom's Broccoli-Rice Casserole   *Amanda Constantino*
Oviedo, FL

*When I was a child, my mom used to make this dish for
every holiday and special occasion. She shared the recipe with
me and now I make it for all our family gatherings too!*

2 to 3 t. oil
1 onion, chopped
2 10-oz. pkgs. frozen chopped
 broccoli, thawed
2 10-3/4 oz. cans cream of
 mushroom soup

2 c. cooked white jasmine rice
1 t. salt
8-oz. pkg. shredded medium
 Cheddar cheese, divided

Heat oil in a large saucepan over medium heat. Add onion and
broccoli; cook for about 5 minutes, until heated through. Add soup and
bring to a boil, stirring constantly. Reduce heat to low. Stir in cooked
rice, salt and cheese, reserving 1/3 cup cheese for topping. Cook until
melted. Spread mixture in a lightly greased 13"x9" baking pan;
sprinkle reserved cheese on top. Bake, uncovered, at 350 degrees for
20 minutes, or until bubbly and heated through. Serves 10 to 12.

Fresh vegetables are delicious and nutritious, but only if
they're used promptly, so don't hesitate to use frozen vegetables
instead. Microwave them quickly or add them, still frozen,
to a simmering pot of soup or a boiling pasta pot.

TASTY
Salads & Sides

Spinach Casserole

Kay Daugherty
Collinsville, MS

This yummy casserole is expected at every family gathering!

2 10-oz. pkgs. frozen chopped
    spinach, thawed and drained
salt and pepper to taste
10-3/4 oz. can cream of
    mushroom soup
8-oz. container sour cream

3/4 c. frozen chopped pepper,
    onion & celery mix
1/2 sleeve round buttery
    crackers, crushed
3 eggs, beaten
2 c. shredded Cheddar cheese,
    divided

Place spinach in a large bowl; season with salt and pepper. Combine
remaining ingredients, reserving 1/2 cup cheese. Pour mixture into a
lightly greased 2-quart casserole dish. Bake, uncovered, at 350 degrees
for 45 minutes, or until center is set. Top with remaining cheese. Bake
for an additional 10 minutes, or until cheese is melted. Serves 8 to 10.

Turnip Greens with Bacon

Courtney Stultz
Weir, KS

*Don't let those turnip greens go to waste! Turn them into
a delicious side dish with just a few extra ingredients.*

3 slices bacon
2 T. coconut oil
6 c. turnip greens, trimmed
1/2 c. onion, sliced

1 t. garlic, minced
1 t. sea salt
1/2 t. pepper

In a large skillet over medium heat, cook bacon until crisp. Remove
bacon from skillet; drain on paper towels. Add oil to drippings in
skillet; add remaining ingredients. Cook, stirring often, until greens
are soft and cooked through. Crumble bacon and return to skillet.
Stir to combine and serve. Makes 4 servings.

Gently scrub vegetables with a damp
sponge sprinkled with baking soda...it
works just as well as pricey cleansers.

69

Hearty Lima Bean Casserole

Marilyn Gabler
Fort Worth, TX

I like to use fresh herbs from my herb garden in this original recipe.
Chock-full of sour cream and cheese, it's a great cool-weather dish.

2 c. dried lima beans
2 c. vegetable broth
1 c. water
1/2 yellow onion, diced
8-oz. container fat-free
    sour cream

garlic powder to taste
chopped fresh oregano to taste
Garnish: 1/2 c. shredded
    Cheddar cheese

Place dried beans in a 4-quart slow cooker; add broth and water.
Cover and cook on high setting for about 4 hours. Reduce heat to low;
continue cooking for 2 hours, or until beans are tender but not mushy.
If too dry, add a little more broth. Drain beans; transfer to a greased
3-quart casserole dish. Add onion, sour cream and seasonings; top
with cheese. Bake, uncovered, at 375 degrees for 30 minutes, or until
hot and bubbly. Serves 4.

Dried beans are nutritious, inexpensive and come in lots of
varieties...perfect for delicious family meals. Before cooking,
place beans in a colander, rinse well and pick through,
discarding any small twigs or bits of debris.

TASTY
Salads & Sides

Redskin Potato Bake

Jo Ann Belovitch
Stratford, CT

Bake this simple potato casserole alongside a chicken as it roasts, for a wonderful meal without much effort.

6 redskin potatoes, thinly sliced
1/2 c. onion, thinly sliced
1/2 c. butter, melted

1/2 t. red pepper flakes
salt to taste

Arrange potatoes and onion in an ungreased 9"x9" baking pan. Combine melted butter and seasonings; drizzle over top. Cover with aluminum foil. Bake at 400 degrees for 25 minutes. Uncover and bake 15 to 20 minutes longer, until potatoes are tender. Makes 4 servings.

D's Cheesy Tots

Deanna Owen
Louisville, KY

One day I needed a side dish for a family get-together and decided to make my own version of hashbrown casserole. Today, I am not allowed to show up to some family gatherings without this cheesy yummy dish!

30-oz. pkg. frozen potato
  rounds, thawed
10-3/4 oz. can cream of
  chicken soup

1.35-oz. pkg. onion soup mix
1/2 c. plus 2 T. milk
8-oz. pkg. sharp shredded
  Cheddar cheese, divided

In a large bowl, mix potatoes, soup, soup mix, milk and half of cheese. Mix gently until well blended. Transfer mixture to a 12"x9" baking pan sprayed with non-stick vegetable spray. Sprinkle remaining cheese on top. Bake, uncovered, at 350 degrees for 30 minutes, or until bubbly and golden. Makes 8 to 10 servings.

Making baked potatoes for the whole family? Stand 'em up
in a muffin pan...easy in and out of the oven.

71

Easy Panzanella Salad

Kaela Oates
Waverly, WV

I came up with this recipe one day when I had ripe tomatoes and cucumber to use up. It's delicious! Easy to double or triple for a crowd...perfect for a picnic.

2 ripe tomatoes, chopped
1 cucumber, peeled and chopped
1 c. seasoned croutons

Italian garlic-basil salad
dressing to taste

Combine all ingredients in a serving bowl; stir gently. Let stand for one to 2 hours before serving. Serves 2 to 4.

Homemade salad croutons are simple to make and a great way to use up day-old bread. Melt 1/4 cup butter in a skillet over medium heat. Stir in 3 cups of bread cubes and toss to coat. Cook, stirring occasionally, until crisp and golden. Season with salt or pepper, if desired.

TASTY
Salads & Sides

Italian Spiral Pasta Salad

Alyssa McIntosh
Lexington, KY

This delicious salad adapts easily to whatever veggies you have on hand and it's easily doubled. Other tasty additions include green, red or yellow peppers, artichokes, sun-dried tomatoes, green onions, fresh basil and fresh mozzarella cheese. Dice ingredients for easy serving.

16-oz. pkg. tri-colored spiral
    pasta, uncooked
4-oz. jar sliced green olives,
    drained

1 c. grape tomatoes, halved
8-oz. bottle Italian dressing
shredded Parmesan cheese
    to taste

Cook pasta according to package directions; drain and rinse with cold water. Transfer pasta to a bowl; add olives and tomatoes. Toss with enough salad dressing to thoroughly coat salad; cover and chill. Top with cheese before serving. Makes 4 to 6 servings.

Tortellini 3-Bean Salad

Lorna Hayes
Roseville, CA

This salad makes a great side dish or a light summer supper. Never any leftovers with this dish!

9-oz. pkg. cheese tortellini,
    uncooked
2 15-oz. cans 3-bean salad
8-oz. pkg. cotto salami, cut into
    thin ribbons

2 5-oz. pkgs. baby spinach
Garnish: grated Parmesan
    cheese

Cook pasta according to package directions; drain and transfer to a bowl. While still warm, add undrained 3-bean salad and salami; set aside. To serve, arrange spinach in a large serving dish, or on individual salad plates. Spoon tortellini mixture onto spinach by large spoonfuls. Sprinkle with cheese. Makes 6 to 8 servings.

Pick up a vintage divided serving dish...just right for serving up a choice of sides without crowding the table.

Cold Spaghetti Salad

Pattie Impens
Ontario, Canada

Once my late husband came home from a party and told me all about this salad and how delicious it was. He was right!

16-oz. pkg. spaghetti, uncooked
2 to 3 ripe tomatoes, diced
1 green pepper, diced
seasoning salt, salt and pepper
    to taste

16-oz. bottle Italian salad
    dressing, divided
1 c. shredded Cheddar or
    marble cheese

Cook spaghetti according to package directions; drain and rinse with cold water. Transfer to a bowl; cover and chill for 2 hours. Add tomatoes, green pepper, seasonings and desired amount of salad dressing. Mix well; add cheese and mix again. Cover and refrigerate until serving time. Add more salad dressing before serving, if desired. Serves 8 to 10.

My Sister's Pasta Salad

Judy Taylor
Butler, MO

My sister Jane used to make this tasty salad for our family reunions and everyone enjoyed it. We lost her to cancer 8 years ago. Now when I make this salad, it is always with thoughts of her.

12-oz. pkg. tri-colored spiral
    pasta, uncooked
3/4 c. onion, chopped
2 c. Cheddar cheese, cubed

1-1/2 c. salted roasted peanuts
12-oz. bottle poppy seed salad
    dressing

Cook pasta according to package directions; drain and rinse with cold water. Transfer pasta to a bowl; add onion, cheese and peanuts. Pour dressing over all; mix well. Cover and refrigerate for 6 hours or overnight, for flavors to blend. Makes 8 servings.

The right garnish can make a plain salad special...make a great salad spectacular! Try a sprinkle of toasted sesame seeds, chopped nuts or sunflower kernels for extra texture, and a sprinkle of snipped fresh chives or basil for flavor.

Angel Hair Pasta Salad

Carolyn Gochenaur
Howe, IN

This recipe was shared with me by a fellow Home Extension homemaker. It is so good and easy to make.

8-oz. pkg angel hair pasta,
    uncooked
3 cucumbers, diced

1 bunch green onions, sliced
1 to 3 T. dill weed
15-oz. jar coleslaw dressing

Cook pasta according to package directions; drain and rinse with cold water. Transfer pasta to a serving bowl; add vegetables, dill weed and coleslaw dressing. Mix, using your hands or a large spoon. Cover and refrigerate until ready to serve. Makes 10 to 12 servings.

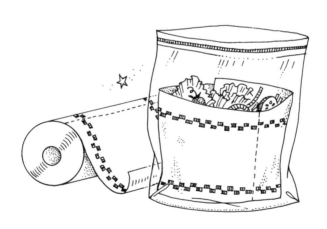

Store salad greens in a plastic zipping bag, tuck in a paper towel to absorb extra moisture and refrigerate. They'll stay crisp for up to 4 days.

Blue Cheese Coleslaw

Roberta Simpkins
Mentor on the Lake, OH

*I tasted this coleslaw at a cookout several years ago and it was
so delicious! I asked for the recipe before I left. Now I never
plan a summer cookout without it.*

1 head cabbage, shredded
1 lb. bacon, chopped and
    crisply cooked
1 red onion, diced

2 4-oz. pkgs. crumbled
    blue cheese
15-oz. jar coleslaw dressing

Combine all ingredients in a large serving bowl. Toss gently to mix.
Cover and chill several hours before serving. Serves 10 to 12.

Pineapple Coleslaw

Edward Kielar
Whitehouse, OH

A tasty variation on coleslaw that goes well with fish and chicken.

1 head cabbage, chopped
2 carrots, peeled and grated
15-oz. jar coleslaw dressing

15-1/4 oz. can crushed
    pineapple, drained
salt and pepper to taste

In a large serving bowl, mix cabbage and carrots with salad dressing.
Add pineapple; season to taste. Cover and chill. Makes 10 servings.

Look for shredded coleslaw mix in the produce section...
it eliminates the time you'd normally take to rinse and chop
cabbage. Broccoli slaw mix is another handy choice.

Sunshine Carrot Salad

Janis Parr
Ontario, Canada

With its appealing color and different texture, this quick recipe is so yummy. It makes a nice extra dish for your buffet table.

4 carrots, peeled and grated
1 T. mayonnaise
1/4 t. salt
1/8 t. pepper
1/2 c. raisins
Garnish: lettuce leaves

In a bowl, stir together carrots, mayonnaise and seasonings. Fold in raisins. Spoon mixture into a salad bowl lined with lettuce leaves. Cover and chill for 2 hours. Serves 4.

Mexican Carrots

Judy Borecky
Escondido, CA

These cool and spicy carrots are something a little different for your taco night dinner.

2 lbs. carrots, peeled and sliced
    on the diagonal
4-oz. can diced jalapeño peppers
1 onion, thinly sliced
2 T. oil
1 c. white vinegar
salt and pepper to taste

In a saucepan, cover carrots with water. Cook over medium-high heat just until tender; drain. In a serving bowl, combine carrots, jalapeño peppers with juice and remaining ingredients; mix all together. Cover and chill at least 3 hours. Serves 6 to 8.

Whip up a zippy Tex-Mex side dish pronto! Prepare instant rice, using chicken broth instead of water. Stir in a generous dollop of spicy salsa, top with shredded cheese and cover with a lid for a few minutes, until the cheese is melted.

Herbed Oven Potatoes

Mel Chencharick
Julian, PA

I love fried potatoes...these are baked, so they're a little healthier than fried, I'm always looking for a recipe to give them a little extra flavor and these simple seasonings do that. Great with any meat you serve...perfect for a picnic or a covered dish get-together.

1/2 t. dried basil
1/2 t. dried thyme
1/2 t. salt
1/2 t. pepper
5 T. butter, melted and divided

2 lbs. red or white potatoes, peeled, very thinly sliced and divided
6 T. onion, finely chopped and divided

Combine seasonings in a cup; set aside. In a large cast-iron skillet or oven-safe skillet, spread 2 tablespoons melted butter. Layer with 1/3 of the potatoes, 1/3 of seasoning mixture, 4 teaspoons melted butter and 2 tablespoons onion. Repeat layers 2 more times. Cover tightly with aluminum foil. Bake at 425 degrees for 20 minutes. Uncover; bake about 25 minutes more, until potatoes are tender. Makes 6 to 8 servings.

Potatoes come in 3 types. Starchy russet potatoes bake up fluffy and are great for frying too. Round waxy potatoes are excellent in soups, casseroles and potato salads. All-purpose potatoes are in between and work well in most recipes. Do some delicious experimenting to find your favorites!

TASTY
Salads & Sides

Potatoes Dijon

Shirley Howie
Foxboro, MA

These potatoes are so easy to make and are a healthy alternative to fried potatoes. They're full-flavored and are a perfect side dish to just about anything. I often substitute other herbs like thyme or rosemary for the Italian seasoning.

3 T. Dijon mustard
2 T. olive oil
1 clove garlic, minced

1/2 t. Italian seasoning
2 lbs. red potatoes, cut into
   bite-size chunks

In a large bowl, mix mustard, olive oil, garlic and seasoning until well blended. Add potatoes; stir until well coated. Spread potatoes out evenly in a 13"x9" baking pan with non-stick vegetable spray. Bake, uncovered, at 425 degrees for 35 to 40 minutes, until potatoes are tender and golden, stirring occasionally. Serves 6.

Roasted Okra Fries

Sonia Hawkins
Amarillo, TX

I love okra cooked this way and it is healthier than fried okra! We use this recipe to roast cauliflower, broccoli, zucchini, yellow squash and Brussels sprouts. Asparagus too...sprinkle with 1/4 cup grated Parmesan cheese the last 5 minutes of roasting. Yum!

1 lb. fresh okra
2 T. olive oil

1/4 t. garlic powder
salt and pepper to taste

Rinse okra and pat dry with a paper towel. Trim off stem ends; cut okra into slices and place in a large bowl. Drizzle with olive oil and toss to coat well. Sprinkle with seasonings. Spread okra on an oiled 17"x12" jelly-roll pan. Bake at 425 degrees for 20 minutes, or until okra is crisp and golden. Serves 4.

For a quick & tasty side, slice ripe tomatoes in half and sprinkle with minced garlic, Italian seasoning and Parmesan cheese. Broil until tender, about 5 minutes.

Asparagus & New Potatoes

Theresa Jakab
Milford, CT

The kids like this and devour it every time! Springtime flavors...
super-easy and delicious. In the summer, top with chopped
fresh parsley or basil from the garden.

1 bunch fresh asparagus with
   thick stalks, ends trimmed
1 to 2 lbs. new potatoes,
   quartered or halved
2 to 3 T. olive oil

3 cloves garlic, minced
1 T. Italian seasoning
kosher salt and pepper to taste
Garnish: shredded Parmesan
   cheese

Cut asparagus into 1-1/2 to 2-inch pieces. In a very large bowl, toss
asparagus, potatoes, olive oil, garlic and seasoning. Season generously
with salt and pepper. May use use your hands to rub the oil and
seasonings into the vegetables. Spread vegetables evenly in a greased
shallow 13"x9" baking pan. Bake, uncovered, at 400 degrees for 35 to
45 minutes, until potatoes are tender. Serve with Parmesan cheese.
Serves 5.

June 17 is National Eat Your Vegetables Day...a great day to let
the kids try some new veggies! Try tempting them with steamed,
chilled baby-size vegetables and a favorite dip like hummus,
ranch dressing or peanut butter.

Roasted Broccolini & Asparagus

Jasmine Burgess
DeWitt, MI

I like to serve this fresh vegetable dish in the summer with grilled salmon for a light yet satisfying meal.

1-1/2 T. garlic-flavored or
    plain extra virgin olive oil
1/2 t. garlic-herb seasoning
    blend
1/4 t. salt
1 bunch asparagus, trimmed

1 bunch broccolini, trimmed
    and split
1/2 c. green onions, sliced
Garnish: shredded Parmesan
    cheese to taste

Combine oil and seasonings in a deep bowl. Add vegetables; toss to coat. Spread evenly onto a parchment paper-lined baking sheet. Bake at 350 degrees for 25 minutes. Remove from oven; sprinkle with cheese. Serve immediately. Serves 4 to 6.

Roasted Cauliflower with Parmesan

Lisa Ann Panzino DiNunzio
Vineland, NJ

A simply delicious side dish that's sure to disappear quickly!

1 head cauliflower, cut into
    1-inch flowerets
3 to 4 T. extra virgin olive oil
1/2 c. Italian-flavored dry
    bread crumbs

1/4 c. grated Parmesan cheese
garlic powder, salt and pepper
    to taste

In a bowl, toss cauliflower with olive oil, bread crumbs and cheese. Spread in a single layer on a rimmed baking sheet coated with non-stick vegetable spray. Season with garlic powder, salt and pepper. Bake at 400 degrees for 25 to 35 minutes, until golden. Makes 4 to 6 servings.

Roasted vegetables are delicious served hot as a side dish or chopped and chilled for a salad topper.

Zucchini Creole

Patricia Nau
River Grove, IL

I've been making this dish for over 40 years. We used to take it to our parish potluck...always a winner!

2 lbs. zucchini, sliced
  1/4-inch thick
3 T. butter
1 onion, chopped
1 clove garlic, pressed
4 ripe tomatoes, cut into wedges

seasoned salt or kosher salt
  to taste
pepper or lemon pepper
  seasoning to taste
Garnish: grated Parmesan or
  Romano cheese

In a skillet over medium heat, sauté zucchini in butter. Add onion and garlic; cook and stir for about 10 minutes, until tender. Add tomatoes and seasonings. Cover and simmer for 20 minutes, stirring occasionally. Sprinkle with cheese just before serving. If preferred, spoon sautéed mixture into a 3-quart casserole dish, sprinkling cheese on top. Bake, uncovered, at 350 degrees for 30 to 35 minutes. Makes 6 servings.

Skillet Tomatoes, Zucchini & Squash

Ramona Storm
Gardner, IL

A great way to use the fresh vegetables from your garden or a nearby farmers' market. Goes together quickly!

1 T. olive oil
1 zucchini, sliced
1 yellow squash, sliced

1/2 c. onion, sliced
14-1/2 oz. can Italian-style
  diced tomatoes

Heat oil in a skillet over medium heat; add zucchini, squash and onion. Cook until tender, stirring occasionally. Add tomatoes with juice; cover and heat through. Makes 4 servings.

Add a little butter to the oil when sautéing...it helps foods cook up golden and adds delicious flavor.

Squash Au Gratin

LaDeana Cooper
Batavia, OH

I'm always looking at new ways to fix things to keep up the kids' interest in yummy vegetables. I have been using this one for awhile now and some friends begged me to make it for their family gathering. It makes an excellent light side for any gathering, especially during those hot summer months.

1 c. seasoned dry bread crumbs
1/4 c. grated Parmesan cheese
1/2 t. salt
1/2 t. pepper
2 zucchini, halved lengthwise
   and sliced 1/4-inch thick

2 yellow squash, halved
   lengthwise and sliced
   1/4-inch thick
2 to 3 T. olive oil

In a gallon-size plastic zipping bag, mix bread crumbs, cheese and seasonings. Add zucchini and squash to the bag; shake very well to coat with seasoned crumbs. Arrange squash and zucchini alternately in a lightly greased 13"x9" baking pan, making 3 to 4 rows and overlapping slightly. Sprinkle with any remaining crumbs left in bag. Lightly drizzle with olive oil. Cover; bake at 350 degrees for 20 to 30 minutes, just until tender. Makes 8 servings.

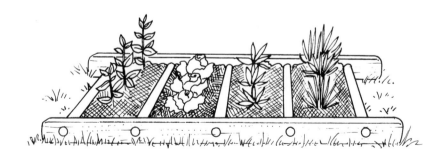

What was Paradise but a garden, full of vegetables
and herbs and pleasures?
– William Lawson

Family Favorite

Lisa's Pineapple Croissant Bake

Lisa Hains
Ontario, Canada

A wonderful side with ham! So fast and simple...a delightful side you'll be happy to serve it to company as well as family.

4 eggs, beaten
1-1/4 c. sugar
20-oz. can crushed pineapple

6 c. croissants, cubed
1/2 c. butter, cubed

In a bowl, combine eggs, sugar and pineapple with juice. Mix well; fold in croissants. Spoon into a greased 13"x9" baking pan. Dot with butter. Bake, uncovered, at 350 degrees for one hour, or until golden. Serve warm. Makes 6 to 8 servings.

Alice's Brown Sugared Apricots

JoAlice Patterson-Welton
Lawrenceville, GA

A family favorite! This is a recipe my late mother conjured up in the kitchen one day as she was looking for a different kind of side dish for the baked chicken dinner she was cooking. I am blessed that my mom was a wonderful Southern cook.

3 17-oz. cans sliced apricots,
    drained
1 sleeve round buttery
    crackers, crushed

1 c. light brown sugar, packed
1/2 c. butter, melted

Arrange apricots in a lightly greased 13"x9" baking pan. Combine crushed crackers with brown sugar; crumble over apricots. Drizzle with melted butter. Bake, uncovered, at 300 degrees for 40 minutes. Serve warm. Makes 6 to 8 servings.

When the recipe calls for cracker crumbs, seal crackers in a plastic zipping bag, then crush with a rolling pin. No mess!

FAMILY-PLEASING
Mains

Easy Yum-Yum Chicken

Brenda Rogers
Atwood, CA

This tasty, super-easy chicken uses only a few ingredients and is a healthy slow-cooker favorite for busy weeknights. I serve this with jasmine rice.

2 T. olive oil
3 T. garlic paste or minced garlic
4 chicken thighs

2 t. salt-free seasoning blend
1/2 c. balsamic vinegar

Add olive oil and garlic to a 3-quart slow cooker; stir together and spread around in the bottom. Place chicken in slow cooker; sprinkle with seasoning. Drizzle balsamic vinegar over chicken. Cover and cook on high setting for about 4 hours, until chicken is tender. Serves 4.

Chicken & Gravy

Debbie White
Williamson, WV

My husband is a very picky eater, but this is one dish that he really likes. The chicken comes out so juicy and tender. It's easily doubled or tripled in a larger slow cooker. Serve with mashed potatoes, noodles or rice.

2 to 4 boneless, skinless chicken
    breasts, fat trimmed

10-1/2 oz. can chicken gravy

Spray a 3-quart slow cooker with cooking spray; add chicken breasts. Pour gravy over chicken. Cover and cook on low setting for 5 to 6 hours, until chicken is very tender. Serves 2 to 4.

Beginning a speedy supper? Check the recipe first, to make sure you have everything on hand before you begin...no last-minute trips to the store for a forgotten ingredient!

Laura's Chicken Diable

Pamela Myers
Auburn, IN

My sister-in-law is a fabulous cook. She has shared many delicious recipes with me over the years, and this one is a favorite! It comes together so quickly and clean-up is a breeze because everything is prepared in one pan. The original recipe calls for a teaspoon of curry powder, but I've always left it out.

1/4 c. butter, melted	1 t. salt
1/2 c. honey	4 to 6 boneless, skinless
1/4 c. mustard	chicken breasts

Spread butter in a shallow 13"x9" baking pan; stir in honey, mustard and salt. Pat chicken dry; roll in butter mixture to coat both sides. Arrange chicken in a single layer in the same pan. Bake, uncovered, at 375 degrees for one hour, or until chicken is tender and richly glazed. Makes 4 to 6 servings.

Use acrylic paint to write "Today's Specials" across the top of a chalkboard. Use chalk to update daily...let everyone know what's for dinner!

Tempting Teriyaki Chicken

Amy Holt
Enterprise, UT

I have to triple this recipe when I make it for my family...
they absolutely love it.

2/3 c. soy sauce
1/3 c. sugar
1/4 t. ground ginger
1/8 t. garlic powder

4 to 5 boneless, skinless chicken
  breasts
cooked rice
Garnish: sliced green onions,
  sesame seed

In a large skillet over medium heat, whisk together soy sauce, sugar, ginger and garlic powder. When heated through, add chicken. Cover and simmer, basting chicken occasionally with sauce, for about 30 minutes, until chicken is no longer pink in the center. Uncover and cook an additional 10 minutes, or until sauce thickens. Serve with rice; garnish with green onions and sesame seed. Serves 4 to 6.

Aloha Chicken

Shirley Howie
Foxboro, MA

There are lots of different kinds of barbecue sauce, so this slow-cooker recipe is fun to experiment with! Choose your favorite or try a new one. It all goes together very quickly and is always yummy!

4 boneless, skinless chicken
  breasts
8-oz. can crushed pineapple,
  drained

16-oz. bottle barbecue sauce
3 green onions, chopped
cooked rice

Place chicken in a 4-quart slow cooker. Combine pineapple and barbecue sauce; spoon over chicken. Top with onions. Cover and cook on low setting for 6 to 8 hours. Serve chicken over cooked rice. Makes 4 servings.

Chicken thighs are juicy and flavorful. Feel free to substitute them in most recipes that call for chicken breasts.

FAMILY-PLEASING
Mains

Impress-the-Guests Chicken
Dale-Harriet Rogovich
Madison, WI

This recipe allows you two hours to set a fancy table. play with the cat or take a little nap before the guests come! Once in the oven, it needs no attention. Suggestion: Double the sauce ingredients, it's delicious. Serve over rice or thin egg noodles (with lots of sauce) or next to mashed potatoes. Buttered green beans go very well with this dish. Guaranteed to impress...don't let on how easy it is!

6 boneless, skinless chicken
   breasts
6 slices dried beef
12 slices bacon

16-oz. container sour cream
10-3/4 oz. can cream of
   mushroom soup
Optional: paprika

Top each chicken breast with one slice dried beef. Wrap 2 slices bacon around each chicken breast, tucking ends underneath. Arrange chicken breasts in a greased 3-quart casserole dish; set aside. In a bowl, blend together soup and sour cream, blending but not stirring vigorously; spread evenly over chicken. Bake, uncovered, at 325 degrees for 2 hours. Makes 6 servings.

No matter what looms ahead, if you can eat today, enjoy today, mix good cheer with friends today, enjoy it and bless God for it.
– Henry Ward Beecher

Pork Chops, Peas & Rice

Bev MacNeil
Ontario, Canada

A recipe similar to this was given to me as a newlywed over 30 years ago. It has been a staple in our house ever since. Never any leftovers! Substitute cream of chicken soup and chicken breasts for another delicious way to enjoy this recipe.

10-3/4 oz. can cream of
   mushroom soup
1.35-oz. pkg. onion soup mix
15-oz. can peas, drained

1-1/2 c. long-cooking rice,
   uncooked
4 pork chops
3 c. boiling water

In a lightly greased skillet over medium heat, brown pork chops on both sides. Meanwhile, spread soup in a lightly greased roasting pan. Sprinkle soup mix over soup. Spread peas and uncooked rice on top. Arrange browned pork chops over the rice. Pour boiling water over top. Cover and bake at 400 degrees for 55 to 60 minutes. Makes 4 servings.

Sweet-and-Sour Pork Chops

Bethi Hendrickson
Danville, PA

This recipe was a staple when I was growing up. It can be doubled very easily as needed. Set some fresh Parmesan cheese on the table and you have a winner.

4 pork chops
1 c. catsup
1 c. water
2 t. Worcestershire sauce

1/4 c. brown sugar, packed
12-oz. pkg. medium egg
   noodles, cooked

In a lightly greased large skillet over medium heat, brown pork chops on both sides; drain. Mix together remaining ingredients except noodles; spoon over pork chops. Simmer over medium-low heat for one hour. Serve pork chops and sauce over cooked egg noodles. Makes 4 servings.

Keep the pantry tidy...tuck packets of seasoning mix
into a napkin holder.

FAMILY-PLEASING
Mains

Savory Soy Marinade Pork Chops

Paula Weaver
Steeleville, IL

These are yummy! We love to grill outside and are always looking for new ideas. This easy recipe is a favorite.

1/2 c. oil
1/2 c. soy sauce
1/2 c. brown sugar, packed

5 pork chops, one inch thick,
or 5 slices pork loin

Mix oil, soy sauce and brown sugar together in a shallow bowl. Add pork chops; turn to coat. Cover and refrigerate for 2 to 5 hours, turning pork chops over every hour. Drain, discarding marinade. Grill pork chops over medium heat, golden on both sides and cooked through. Makes 5 servings.

Maple Pork Chops

Emma Brown
Saskatchewan, Canada

The sweetness of the maple syrup and saltiness of the soy sauce go together so well, you may want to double this recipe!

1/2 c. maple syrup
3 T. soy sauce
2 cloves garlic, minced

4 thick bone-in pork chops
1 T. oil

In a bowl, whisk together maple syrup, soy sauce and garlic; reserve and refrigerate 1/4 cup of mixture. Add pork chops to remaining mixture in bowl. Cover and refrigerate for at least 15 minutes to overnight, turning pork chops occasionally. Drain, discarding mixture in bowl. Heat oil in a large cast-iron skillet over medium-high heat. Add pork chops. Cook until golden and no longer pink in the center, about 5 minutes per side. At serving time, warm reserved syrup mixture; drizzle over pork chops. Makes 4 servings.

Start family meals with a gratitude circle...everyone takes a moment to share something they're thankful for that day. It's a sure way to put everyone in a cheerful mood!

Ham & Garden Veggies

Candy Foltz
Hagerstown, MD

This is a recipe my family has made for years. It started out as a garden meal, using the veggies that were fresh from Momma & Daddy's garden. I don't have a veggie garden but still use this recipe often after visiting the farmers' market.

5 slices bacon
6 ears corn, cut off the ear, or
   2 15-1/4 oz. cans corn,
   drained
4 c. green beans, snapped, or
   2 14-1/2 oz. cans cut green
   beans, drained

2 c. water
2 c. cooked ham, cubed

In a skillet over medium heat, cook bacon until crisp. Drain, reserving drippings; cool and refrigerate bacon. In a 5-quart slow cooker, combine corn, green beans, water and reserved bacon drippings. Cover and cook on low setting for 3 hours. Add ham; stir. Crumble bacon and sprinkle over top. Turn to high setting; cover and cook 3 more hours. Serves 8 to 10.

Creamy Ham & Beans

Diane Cohen
Breinigsville, PA

No soaking beans required! Just combine everything in the slow cooker, and dinner is ready in a few hours. I like to serve this with warm buttered cornbread.

16-oz. pkg. dried Great
   Northern beans
6 c. chicken broth or water
2 c. cooked ham, cubed

1 t. garlic, minced
2 t. onion powder
salt and pepper to taste

Combine all ingredients in a 5-quart slow cooker; stir. Cover and cook on low setting for 8 hours, or until beans are tender. Makes 6 servings.

Linda's Ham & Sweet Potato Dinner

Linda Smith
Fountain Hills, AZ

This is a wonderful, tasty slow-cooker recipe. We make it during the Christmas holidays. It's a quick & easy and goes well with all the other holiday dishes.

2 to 4 small sweet potatoes
1-1/2 lb. boneless ham

1/4 c. brown sugar, packed
1/2 t. dry mustard

Arrange unpeeled sweet potatoes in a 5-quart slow cooker. Place ham on top of sweet potatoes. Combine brown sugar and mustard in a cup; spread over top of ham. Cover and cook on low setting for 6 hours, or until a meat thermometer inserted in thickest part of ham reads 145 degrees. To serve, remove ham and sweet potatoes to a platter; let cool for a few minutes. Slice ham and sweet potatoes, removing potato skins if desired. Serve with juices from slow cooker spooned over all. Makes 4 servings.

Celebrate Family Day on September 26...let the rest of the family help make dinner! Younger children can tear lettuce for salad, while older kids can measure, chop, stir a skillet and maybe even help with meal planning and shopping. Then enjoy your dinner together as a family.

Chicken Mac & Cheese

Denise Webb
Newington, GA

A dear lady in our church made this for our family when our children were young. They absolutely loved it! When I discovered how quick & easy it was to make, it was a win-win!

1-1/2 c. elbow macaroni,
   uncooked
10-3/4 oz. can cream of
   chicken soup

1 c. milk
1 c. shredded Cheddar cheese
1-1/2 c. cooked chicken,
   chopped

Mix uncooked macaroni and remaining ingredients in an ungreased 2-quart casserole dish. Cover and bake at 350 degrees for one hour. Makes 4 to 6 servings.

Mom's Macaroni with Tomatoes

Sandy Wood
Ryland Heights, KY

My mom always fixed this in the "old days"...it was economical as well as filling. Still is!

2 c. elbow macaroni, uncooked
14-1/2 oz. can diced tomatoes

3/4 c. shredded Cheddar cheese
1 t. butter

Cook macaroni according to package directions. Drain; transfer to a lightly greased one-quart casserole dish. Stir in tomatoes with juice, cheese and butter. Bake, uncovered, at 350 degrees for 30 minutes, or until hot and bubbly. Makes 6 servings.

Wanting to cut calories? Use sharp or extra-sharp cheese in recipes.
You can use a little less cheese without diminishing the flavor.

FAMILY-PLEASING *Mains*

Mac & Cheese for a Crowd

Bea Plumley
Wellsboro, PA

This is my go-to mac & cheese recipe I can just take the ingredients to a neighbor's or family member's home, use their slow cooker and in less than 3 hours, dinner is served. Never any leftovers!

16-oz. pkg. elbow macaroni,
  uncooked
10-3/4 oz. can Cheddar cheese
  soup
2 c. 2% milk

1/4 to 1/2 c. butter
16-oz. pkg. shredded Cheddar
  cheese
salt and pepper to taste

Cook macaroni according to package directions; drain and set aside. In a 5-quart slow cooker, combine soup, milk and butter. Cover and cook on high setting until butter melts; stir until smooth. Add cooked macaroni, cheese, salt and pepper. Turn slow cooker to low setting and cook for 2 to 2-1/2 hours, until cheese melts. Serves 15.

Chris's Spicy Mac & Cheese

Crystal Shook
Catawba, NC

My son Chris loves this macaroni & cheese, and it's so simple!

16-oz. pkg. elbow macaroni,
  uncooked

15-oz. jar queso blanco dip

Cook pasta according to directions; drain and return to pan. Add dip to hot macaroni; stir and serve. Makes 8 to 10 servings.

Prefer to shred cheese yourself?
Place the wrapped block of cheese
in the freezer for 15 minutes...it will
just glide across the grater!

Marinated Flank Steak

Irene Robinson
Cincinnati, OH

*Refrigerating the steaks in a spicy marinade before grilling
really adds to the flavor.*

1-1/3 lb. beef flank steak
2 T. low-sodium soy sauce
2 T. honey
2 T. white vinegar
1-1/2 T. ground ginger

1-1/2 t. garlic powder
1-1/2 t. cinnamon
1-1/2 t. nutmeg
1/4 c. oil
1 onion, chopped

Using a sharp knife, make shallow cuts in steak; set aside. Mix remaining ingredients together in a large plastic zipping bag; add steaks. Refrigerate for at least 24 hours, turning several times. Remove from marinade. Grill or broil for 5 to 10 minutes on each side, until desired doneness. Slice thinly on an angle to serve. Makes 6 servings.

If you're turning on the oven to bake potatoes, why not bake a whole oven full? You can grate them and dice them for hashbrowns, soups or casseroles, slice them for home fries or whip up a quick potato salad!

FAMILY-PLEASING
Mains

Millie's Noodle Casserole

Becky Hartsell Riedesel
Cedar Rapids, IA

My great-aunt made this casserole for us when we visited her.
We begged for the recipe and now it's a family favorite!

12-oz. pkg. frozen homestyle
  egg noodles, uncooked
1 lb. lean ground beef
1/2 c. onion, chopped

10-3/4 oz. can tomato soup
1 c. shredded Cheddar cheese
salt and pepper to taste

Cook noodles according to package directions; drain. Meanwhile, in a skillet over medium heat, brown beef and onion; drain. In a greased 2-quart casserole dish, combine cooked noodles, beef mixture and remaining ingredients; mix gently. Bake, uncovered, at 375 degrees for 25 to 30 minutes, until hot and bubbly. Serves 6.

Delicious Beef Short Ribs

Donna Weidner
Schaumburg, IL

I make this slow-cooker recipe every year for
my dad's birthday...it's so easy and so good!

3 to 4 lbs. beef short ribs
1 sweet onion, sliced
18-oz. jar beef gravy

1-oz. pkg. brown or beef
  gravy mix

Place ribs in a 5-quart slow cooker; place sliced onion on top. Mix gravy and gravy mix in a bowl; spoon over top. Cover and cook on low for 8 to 10 hours. Makes 6 servings.

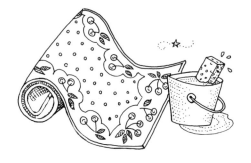

Brightly colored vintage-style oilcloth makes the best-ever tablecloth...it wipes clean in a jiffy!

Skillet Beef Hash

Tyson Ann Trecannelli
Gettysburg, PA

A fast and delicious one-dish meal that's sure to please. They'll be asking for seconds! Serve with corn muffins and a tossed salad, if desired. Serve right from the pan for easy clean-up!

1 to 1-1/2 lbs. lean ground beef
1 onion, halved and thinly sliced
1 green or red pepper, halved
   and thinly sliced
15-oz. can fire-roasted diced
   tomatoes
1-7/8 c. water
1/2 c. long-cooking rice,
   uncooked
2 t. salt
1/4 t. pepper
Optional: 1 to 2 t. chili powder

In an oven-proof skillet with a lid, brown beef over medium heat; drain. Add onion and pepper; sauté until onion is translucent. Stir in uncooked rice, tomatoes with juice, water and seasonings; heat through. Cover and bake at 350 degrees for one hour. Makes 4 to 6 servings.

If your favorite non-stick skillet is sticky, fill it with one cup water, 1/2 cup vinegar and 2 tablespoons baking soda. Bring to a boil for a few minutes. Rinse well with hot water and wipe clean...no more stickiness!

FAMILY-PLEASING
Mains

Margo's Creamy Mushroom Steaks
Margaret Combs
Isom, KY

My family loves these tasty steaks with mashed potatoes,
green beans and coleslaw.

6 to 8 beef cube steaks
salt and pepper to taste
2 c. self-rising flour
1/2 c. shortening

2 10-3/4 oz. cans cream of
    mushroom soup
1 c. milk, or more if needed

Season steaks with salt and pepper; roll in flour and set aside. Melt shortening in a large non-stick skillet over medium heat. Cook steaks until golden and and no longer pink in the center. Remove steaks to a plate. Drain most of shortening, leaving some drippings in skillet. Combine soup with milk and stir well; pour into skillet Cook and stir until gravy is lightly golden. Ladle gravy over steaks. Makes 6 to 8 servings.

Nona's Grandchildren's Special Meatballs
Eleanor Dionne
Beverly, MA

My mom used to make this simple recipe for her grandchildren and they really liked it. It was special because it was served only to the children...the adults were not allowed to eat this! Mom has been gone for a long time, but I continue this tradition with my own grandchildren.

1 lb. ground beef
1/2 c. soft bread crumbs
1/4 c. grated Parmesan cheese

salt and pepper to taste
2 c. tomato sauce
10-oz. pkg. frozen peas

In a large bowl, combine beef, bread crumbs, cheese, salt and pepper. Mix well; form into tiny meatballs. Brown meatballs in a skillet over medium heat; drain. Stir in tomato sauce and peas; cook over low heat for 10 to 15 minutes. Makes 4 servings.

Easy Burrito Casserole

Angela Lively
Conroe, TX

This dish is so easy and really good...great for dinner on a busy night! Use your favorite frozen burritos and canned chili, along with any extra toppings you like.

2 c. refried black beans
8 frozen burritos, completely
  thawed
10-1/2 oz. can red enchilada
  sauce

15-oz. can chili
8-oz. pkg. shredded Monterey
  Jack cheese

Spread beans in a greased 13"x9" baking pan. Arrange thawed burritos on top of beans. In a bowl, mix enchilada sauce and chili together. Spoon sauce mixture over burritos; top with cheese. Bake, uncovered, at 375 degrees for 30 minutes, or until bubbly and burritos are cooked through. Makes 8 servings.

Carnitas Pork Tacos

Geneva Rogers
Gillette, WY

Delicious...and almost no work at all!

3 to 4-lb. boneless pork
  shoulder butt roast, halved
1-1/4 oz. pkg. taco seasoning
  mix
10-oz. can diced tomatoes and
  green chiles

12 8-inch flour tortillas, warmed
8-oz. pkg. shredded Mexican-
  blend cheese
Optional: sour cream

Place roast in a 5-quart slow cooker. Sprinkle with taco seasoning; pour tomatoes with juice over top. Cover and cook on low setting for 6 to 8 hours, until tender. Remove roast from slow cooker; shred with 2 forks. Skim fat from cooking juices. Return shredded pork to slow cooker; heat through. To serve, use a slotted spoon to top tortillas with pork mixture; top with cheese. Serve with sour cream, if desired. Makes 12 servings.

FAMILY-PLEASING
Mains

Mexican Lasagna

Lisanne Miller
Canton, MS

A very flexible recipe...you can easily make multiple trays for a crowd.
Use your favorite salsa...mine is peach. Serve with sour cream,
guacamole, black olives or your favorite toppings.

16-oz. jar salsa, divided
8 to 10 burrito-size soft
    flour tortillas
2 16-oz. cans refried beans
16-oz. pkg. shredded Mexican-
    blend cheese, divided

Optional: 10-oz. can sweet corn
    with diced peppers or black
    beans, drained

Spread a layer of salsa in a lightly greased 13"x9" baking pan; set
aside. Fill the center of each tortilla with refried beans and cheese; do
not overfill. Fold up burrito-style. Arrange burritos in the pan, fitting
tightly. Top with remaining cheese and salsa; add corn or beans, if
desired. Cover with aluminum foil. Bake at 350 degrees for 35 to
40 minutes, until bubbly. Makes 8 to 10 servings.

Candlelight and the good china aren't just for the holidays or special
celebrations...use them to brighten everyday family meals!

Poppy Seed Chicken

Connie Gabbard
Athens, OH

Don't be tempted to sprinkle on the cracker-crumb mixture while the chicken is in the slow cooker...condensation will make the topping soggy.

6 boneless, skinless chicken
  breasts
2 10-3/4 oz. cans cream of
  chicken soup
1 c. milk

1 T. poppy seed
36 round buttery crackers,
  crushed
1/4 c. butter, melted

Place chicken in a lightly greased 5-quart slow cooker. Whisk together soup, milk and poppy seed in a bowl; spoon over chicken. Cover and cook on high setting for one hour. Reduce heat to low setting; cover and cook for 3 hours. Combine cracker crumbs and butter in a bowl, stirring until crumbs are moistened. Sprinkle over chicken just before serving. Makes 6 servings.

Delaware Chicken

Lori Schwander
North East, MD

My family has been making this dish for 40 years! We get together as often as we can. This is a favorite because it is easy and can be prepared ahead of time, to bake while everyone is socializing.

1.35-oz. pkg. onion soup mix
1 c. long-cooking rice, uncooked
10-3/4 oz. can golden
  mushroom soup

2-1/2 c. water
3-1/2 lb. roasting chicken,
  cut into 8 pieces

Sprinkle soup mix in a buttered 13"x9" baking pan. Sprinkle uncooked rice evenly in pan. In a small saucepan over low heat, mix soup and water until smooth. Pour half of soup mixture carefully over rice. Layer chicken in pan; top with remaining soup mixture. Bake, uncovered, at 325 degrees for 90 minutes to one hour and 15 minutes, until rice is tender and soup is absorbed. Serves 4 to 6.

Fiesta Chicken

Rachel Harter
The Woodlands, TX

*I created this recipe on a whim with ingredients I had
on hand. This dish is a healthy southwestern take on chicken,
and it's so easy to prepare!*

4 to 6 boneless, skinless
  chicken breasts
15-1/4 oz. can corn, drained
15-1/2 oz. can black beans,
  drained and rinsed

16-oz. jar salsa
Optional: 7-oz. pkg. Spanish
  rice mix, prepared
Garnish: shredded cheese,
  sliced avocado

Spray a 5-quart slow cooker with non-stick vegetable spray. Arrange
chicken breasts in slow cooker; top with corn, beans and salsa. Cover
and cook on low setting for 7 to 8 hours, or on high setting for
4 hours. Stir just before serving. If desired, serve over Spanish rice;
garnish as desired. Makes 4 servings.

"Fried" ice cream is a fun & festive ending to a Mexican meal. Roll
scoops of ice cream in a mixture of crushed frosted corn flake cereal
and cinnamon. Garnish with a drizzle of honey and a dollop of
whipped topping. They'll ask for seconds!

Chicken & Rice Casserole

Kimberly Lyons
Commerce, TX

Great with fresh-baked bread and a green salad.

2 6.2-oz. pkgs. quick-cooking
   long-grain and wild rice with
   seasoning packets
4 boneless, skinless chicken
   breasts, cooked and cut into
   1-inch cubes

3 10-3/4-oz. cans cream of
   mushroom soup
1-1/3 c. frozen mixed
   vegetables, thawed
3 c. water

Gently stir together all ingredients. Spread into an ungreased 13"x9"
baking pan. Bake, uncovered, at 350 degrees about 45 minutes,
stirring occasionally. Serves 6 to 8.

Country Smothered Chicken Tenders

Debra Caraballo
Humble, TX

*I came up with this quick & easy dinner based on a similar dish
I had at a favorite restaurant of ours in Bryan, Texas that's
no longer in business. We all love this dish.*

8 to 10 frozen uncooked breaded
   chicken tenders
12-oz. pkg. frozen sliced onions
   and green peppers, divided

2-3/4 oz. pkg. country gravy
   mix
2 c. water

Arrange chicken tenders in a 2-quart casserole dish sprayed with
non-stick vegetable spray. Bake, uncovered, at 350 degrees for
20 minutes. Remove from oven. Arrange half of onions and peppers
on top; set aside. Reserve remaining vegetables for another recipe. Stir
together gravy mix and water, blending well; spoon over casserole.
Cover and bake for another 25 to 30 minutes, until chicken and
vegetables are tender and gravy has thickened. Serves 4 to 6.

Rosemary Roast Chicken

Kristy Wells
Ocala, FL

I've been making this dish for my family for years! It's a go-to recipe that everyone loves and it is incredibly easy. The delicious smell from your kitchen will make your neighbors hungry and even the pickiest eaters at the dinner table will clean their plates. This recipe is easily adjusted, depending on number of people you're feeding and pieces of chicken preferred.

3 to 5 lbs. chicken thighs and
    drumsticks, boneless and
    skinless if desired
1/2 c. balsamic vinegar
1/2 c. olive oil

2 T. fresh rosemary, chopped,
    or dried rosemary
2 T. onion & garlic herb
    seasoning

Arrange chicken pieces in a lightly greased large roasting pan. May instead use 2 smaller baking pans to avoid crowding. Drizzle vinegar over chicken and toss to coat; repeat with olive oil. Sprinkle with rosemary and seasoning. Bake, uncovered, at 375 degrees for 30 to 45 minutes, until chicken juices run clear and chicken is crisp and golden. Makes 6 to 12 servings.

Friday night is a great time to invite new neighbors to share a meal. Send them home with a gift basket filled with flyers from favorite bakeries and pizza parlors, coupons and local maps...tuck in a package of homemade cookies too. So thoughtful!

Spaghetti Frittata

Patricia Flak
Erie, PA

My husband requests that I cook too much pasta on
"Spaghetti Night" just so I can make this later in the week.
So easy to change up the seasonings to make it your own.

1-1/2 c. hot cooked spaghetti
4 T. butter, divided
3 eggs, beaten
1/3 c. grated Parmesan cheese
2 T. fresh parsley, chopped

1/4 t. salt
1/8 t. pepper
Cajun or Italian seasoning
   to taste

In a large bowl, toss hot spaghetti with 2 tablespoons butter; set aside. In a separate bowl, beat together eggs, cheese and seasonings. Pour over spaghetti; toss to coat. Melt remaining butter in a skillet over medium heat. Add spaghetti mixture and spread evenly in skillet. Cook over low heat until set at the edges. Loosen edges and cook until golden. Turn out onto a plate; return to skillet top-side down, to finish cooking. Cut frittata into wedges to serve. Makes 4 servings.

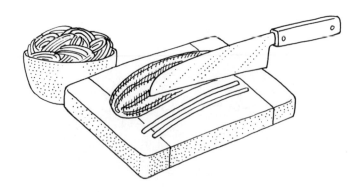

For a healthy change from regular pasta, make "noodles" from zucchini or summer squash. Use a spiralizer or cut the squash into long, thin strips with a knife. Steam lightly or sauté in a little olive oil and toss with your favorite pasta sauce.

FAMILY-PLEASING
Mains

Zesty Tortellini with Feta

Jennifer Rubino
Hickory, NC

*This meatless meal comes together so quickly that it's great
before practice or after the game. Add some fresh fruit
and crusty French bread for a beautiful meal.*

2 9-oz. pkgs. refrigerated
  tortellini or ravioli, uncooked
8-oz. bottle zesty Italian salad
  dressing

8-oz. pkg. pkg. crumbled
  feta cheese
1 c. toasted pine nuts

Cook pasta according to package directions; drain and return to pan.
Add remaining ingredients; stir to coat pasta well. Serve immediately.
Makes 4 servings.

Quick Cheese Tortellini Alfredo

Rebecca Etling
Blairsville, PA

*My husband's new favorite dish! It's also become
one of my favorite last-minute dinners.*

16-oz. pkg. frozen cheese
  tortellini, uncooked
2 15-oz. jars Alfredo sauce
4 to 5 slices bacon, crisply
  cooked and crumbled

1/2 c. grated Parmesan-Romano
  cheese

Cook pasta according to package directions; drain and return to pan.
Add Alfredo sauce; simmer over low heat until warmed through. Serve
garnished with bacon and cheese. Makes 5 to 6 servings.

Sour cream will stay fresh and
tasty longer if you stir in
a teaspoon of white vinegar
after first opening it.

Pineapple Grilled Salmon with Snow Peas

Linda Payne
Snow Hill, MD

Salmon grilled with pineapple is juicy, flavorful and so good for you! On the weekends I always try to cook a batch of brown rice so it's a real time-saver during the week

1 can pineapple rings, drained
    and juice reserved
2 T. soy sauce, divided
1 lb. salmon fillets

1/4 c. water
12-oz. pkg. frozen snow peas,
    thawed
cooked rice

In a glass or plastic dish, pour reserved pineapple juice and one tablespoon soy sauce over salmon. Cover and refrigerate for at least one hour; drain. Grill salmon for 5 minutes on one side; turn. Add pineapple rings to grill. Meanwhile, add water and remaining soy sauce to a sauté pan over medium-high heat. Add snow peas; sauté for 5 to 10 minutes, until crisp-tender. Remove salmon from grill after 5 minutes on the other side; flip pineapple. To serve, divide rice among 4 plates. Top with snow peas and sauce; arrange salmon and pineapple rings on top. Makes 4 servings.

French Onion Rice & Shrimp

Janice Curtis
Yucaipa, CA

I love shrimp, so I'm always trying to come up with new recipes.

3 c. long-cooking rice, uncooked
1/2 lb. uncooked medium
    shrimp, peeled and cleaned
1 c. canned artichoke hearts,
    drained and halved

1-1/2 c. sour cream
1.4-oz. pkg. French onion soup
    mix

Prepare rice according to package directions. Stir shrimp and artichokes into cooked rice. Combine sour cream and soup mix in a bowl; add to rice mixture and stir well. Transfer to a lightly greased 2-quart casserole dish and cover with aluminum foil. Bake at 350 degrees for 45 minutes. Makes 4 servings.

Honey Crumb Haddock

Lisa Breton
North Vassalboro, ME

Once my husband and I went to one of our favorite places to have a quiet date night together. He ordered the honey crumb haddock and loved it. I had a bite and just knew I had to try and make this for him. A few weeks later I made my version of the haddock for dinner. Let's just say, now we have more date nights at home! Be sure to use fresh, unfrozen fish for the best flavor.

1-1/2 lbs. haddock fillets
1 t. garlic powder
1/2 c. butter, melted

1/2 c. honey
1 sleeve round buttery crackers,
　crushed

Arrange fish fillets in a lightly greased 13"x9" baking pan; season with garlic powder. Combine melted butter and honey in a small bowl; mix well and spoon over fish. Top with crushed crackers. Cover and bake at 350 degrees for 30 minutes. Uncover; bake for another 15 minutes. Makes 6 servings.

Lemon Pepper Rainbow Trout

Mary Thomason-Smith
Bloomington, IN

A favorite of my children, this recipe is fast, easy, and healthy... a delicious light meal for any weeknight. Serve with a tossed salad and baked potato for a complete meal.

4 rainbow trout fillets
4 T. butter, melted
1 t. lemon zest

2 T. lemon juice
1 T. lemon pepper seasoning

Preheat broiler on high; position oven rack on level closest to the broiler. Spray an aluminum foil-lined baking sheet lightly with non-stick vegetable spray. Arrange fish fillets on baking sheet; set aside. Combine melted butter, lemon zest and lemon juice; brush over fish. Season with lemon pepper. Broil fish on rack closest to broiler for 5 minutes, or until fish flakes easily. Serves 4.

Easy Sausage, Red Beans & Rice Skillet

Janice Woods
Northern Cambria, PA

A hearty, quick-fix meal to enjoy after a long day. Want more veggies? Stir in some diced onions, green and red peppers when adding the other ingredients to skillet.

1 lb. smoked pork sausage, sliced
2 c. hot cooked white rice
10-oz. can diced tomatoes with green chiles
2 15-1/2 oz. cans red kidney beans, drained and rinsed
1 T. ground cumin
salt and pepper to taste

Spray a large skillet with non-stick vegetable spray. Add sausage and cook over medium heat, stirring often, until lightly browned. Transfer to a plate; cover with aluminum foil and set aside. To same skillet, add cooked rice, tomatoes with juice, beans and cumin; stir to mix well. Cook over medium heat, stirring, until warmed through, about 5 to 7 minutes. Return sausage to pan and season with salt and pepper; heat through. Makes 4 servings.

Italian Sausage Pasta

Nancy Kailihiwa
Wheatland, CA

This is a perfect recipe to share with your family on a chilly day. Serve with a side salad and fresh bread for a hearty and budget-friendly meal.

1 lb. sweet Italian pork sausage links, sliced
1/2 c. water
2 14-1/2 oz. cans diced tomatoes
26-oz. jar favorite pasta sauce
6-1/2 oz. can sliced mushrooms, drained
1 to 2 16-oz. pkgs. favorite pasta, cooked

Brown sausage in a skillet over medium heat. Add water; cook until simmering. Cover and reduce heat to medium-low. Simmer for 15 minutes, stirring occasionally. Add tomatoes with juice; increase heat to medium. Cook, uncovered, until liquid begins to thicken, about 15 minutes. Stir in pasta sauce and mushrooms; heat through. To serve, ladle sauce over cooked pasta. Serves 6.

Smoky Kielbasa with Seasoned Cabbage & Potatoes

Patricia Reitz
Winchester, VA

This recipe was a happy accident! I opened what I thought was a can of sauerkraut, only to find it was actually seasoned cabbage. Completely different product! As it turned out, we loved the meal I made with it and it has since become a family favorite. A complete meal made in one pot in under 30 minutes!

1 T. olive oil
2 lbs. Kielbasa sausage, cut into
    rounds or 3-inch lengths
2 15-oz. cans seasoned cabbage

2 lbs. new redskin potatoes,
    sliced 1/8-inch thick
1/4 t. salt
1/4 t. pepper

Heat olive oil in a very large non-stick skillet over medium heat. Brown Kielbasa on both sides; remove from pan and set aside. Add undrained cabbage to pan. Layer potato slices over cabbage: sprinkle evenly with salt and pepper. Arrange Kielbasa on top of the potatoes. Bring mixture to a boil over medium-high heat. Reduce heat to medium-low and cover pan. Simmer for about 30 minutes, until potatoes are tender. Makes 6 servings.

Cut flowers in a Mason jar are so cheerful on the dinner table! Whether they're from your backyard garden or the grocery store, keep them blooming longer...add a teaspoon of sugar and 1/2 teaspoon of household bleach to the water in the jar.

Mashed Potato & Ham Casserole

Mary Tate
Kansas City, KS

One of my grandson's favorite meals! After a family dinner, I had a lot of mashed potatoes and some pieces of ham left over. So I made up this recipe and it was a hit. It is a delicious way to use leftovers.

3 to 4 c. mashed potatoes
salt and pepper to taste
1/2 to 3/4 c. onion, chopped

2 c. cooked ham, diced
3 c. shredded Swiss cheese

Spread mashed potatoes in a 2-quart microwave-safe casserole dish; season with salt and pepper. Layer with onion, ham and cheese. Cover with plastic wrap or add casserole lid. Microwave on high until heated through and cheese is melted. Serves 3 to 4.

Slow-Cooked Ham Meal

Jenita Davison
La Plata, MO

Creamy comfort food. This smells wonderful while it's cooking!

8 to 12 slices cooked ham, divided
32-oz. pkg. frozen potato puffs, thawed and divided
8-oz. pkg. shredded Cheddar cheese, divided

10-3/4 oz. can cream of mushroom or celery soup, divided
1/2 c. onion, diced and divided
pepper to taste

Spray a 6-quart slow cooker with non-stick vegetable spray. Layer half of each ingredient in the order listed. Repeat layers. Cover and cook on low setting for 6 to 8 hours, or on high setting for 4 hours. (Low setting will not stick as easily.) Stir occasionally along the sides during last half of cooking time. Makes 6 servings.

Sally's Fried Cabbage with Sausage

Sally Davison
Fayette, MO

This is a quick meal that I make almost weekly. When I've traveled to family homes and made this, everyone loves it and wants the easy recipe. It is a no-fail dish.

1/3 to 1/2 c. coconut oil
    or butter
1 head cabbage, shredded,
    or 12-oz. pkg. shredded
    coleslaw mix
1/2 to 3/4 c. onion, chopped

14-1/2 oz. can diced tomatoes,
    plain or with green chiles
1 lb. smoked pork or turkey
    sausage, sliced into rounds
1/2 t. salt
1/2 t. pepper

Melt coconut oil or butter in a large skillet over medium heat. Add cabbage and onion; cook for about 5 minutes, stirring often to prevent sticking. Add tomatoes with juice, sausage and seasonings. Cover and simmer over medium-low heat for 15 to 20 minutes, stirring occasionally. Makes about 8 servings as a side dish, or 2 to 4 as a main dish.

Oops! If a simmering pot starts to burn on the bottom, don't worry. Spoon the unburnt portion into another pan, being careful not to scrape up the scorched part on the bottom. The burnt taste usually won't linger.

Mississippi Roast

Rhi Younts
Richmond, IN

I had been looking for the perfect roast recipe for years and I finally found it! It's so delicious and incredibly easy. I like to serve it with mashed potatoes and if I have some left over, I freeze it for later or make beef and noodles.

1/4 c. water
3-lb. beef chuck roast
1-oz. pkg. au jus gravy mix

1-oz. pkg. ranch salad
 dressing mix
1/2 c. butter, sliced

Pour water into a 6-quart slow cooker; add roast. Sprinkle gravy mix over roast, then salad dressing mix. Dot with slices of butter. Cover and cook on low setting for 6 to 8 hours, until roast is very tender. Shred roast and serve with juices from slow cooker. Makes 6 servings.

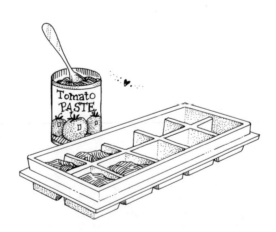

A spoonful or two of tomato paste adds rich flavor to roasts and stews. If you have a partial can left over, freeze the rest in an ice cube tray, then pop out cubes and store in a freezer bag. Frozen cubes can be dropped right into simmering dishes... there's no need to thaw.

FAMILY-PLEASING
Mains

Baked Steak with Gravy

Kathy Van Daalen
New Smyrna Beach, FL

My mother made this often for dinner when I was growing up.
Although she has passed away, it still brings back good
memories and it is truly a comfort food for me.

1 c. all-purpose flour
1/8 t. salt
1/8 t. pepper
6 to 8 beef cube steaks
1 t. butter

2 10-3/4 oz. cans golden
   mushroom soup
2-1/2 c. water
4-oz. can sliced mushrooms,
   drained

Mix flour, salt and pepper in a shallow bowl; dredge steaks in mixture.
Melt butter in a skillet over medium heat; add steaks and brown on
both sides. Arrange steaks in a lightly greased 13"x9" baking pan; set
aside. Stir together soup, water and mushrooms; spoon over steaks.
Cover with aluminum foil. Bake at 325 degrees for 45 to 50 minutes.
Uncover; bake 15 minutes more. Makes 6 to 8 servings.

Salsa Beef

Gina Harrell
Savannah, GA

This delicious dish adds up to more than the sum of its parts...
win-win! Almost no prep time and it's made in a slow cooker.
It has become a family favorite for everyone.

2 lbs. lean stew beef cubes
2 c. favorite salsa
1 T. soy sauce

1 T. brown sugar, packed
Optional: 1 clove garlic, minced
cooked rice

In a 5-quart slow cooker, combine all ingredients except rice. Cover
and cook on low setting for 8 to 10 hours, or high setting for 4 to
5 hours. To serve, ladle beef mixture over cooked rice. Serves 6.

Mix flour and seasonings for dredging
meat on a piece of wax paper...when
you're done, just toss it away.

Melinda's Veggie Stir-Fry

Melinda Daniels
Lewiston, ID

I really like stir-fry and chow mein, so I created this recipe using the items that I had in my garden and fridge. It is now one of my family's favorites and makes great leftovers.

8-oz. pkg. spaghetti, uncooked
2 c. broccoli, cut into bite-size
   flowerets
1 c. snow or sugar snap pea
   pods, halved

2 carrots, peeled and thinly
   sliced
1/2 onion, thinly sliced
1/4 green pepper, thinly sliced

Cook spaghetti as package directs; drain and set aside. Meanwhile, place vegetables into a steamer basket; place in a large stockpot filled with enough water to just reach the bottom of the basket. Cook over medium heat and steam for about 3 to 5 minutes, until just beginning to soften; drain. If crisper vegetables are desired, omit this step. When spaghetti and vegetables are done, add to Stir-Fry Sauce in skillet. Cook and stir over medium-high heat for about 15 minutes, to desired tenderness. Serves 8.

Stir-Fry Sauce:

1/2 c. olive oil
1/3 c. low-sodium soy sauce
2 T. Dijon mustard

2 T. sliced pepperoncini, chopped
2 cloves garlic, minced
1 t. pepper

In a large skillet over low heat, mix all ingredients together. Simmer until sauce is heated through.

FAMILY-PLEASING *Mains*

Easy Baked Ziti

Stephanie Wren
La Vergne, TN

This recipe is super-simple to toss together...and my family loves it!
I prefer provolone over mozzarella in Italian dishes because I think
it has more flavor. You can double this recipe if you have a deep
13"x9" pan or 4-quart casserole.

3 c. penne pasta, uncooked
1 lb. ground beef
1 to 2 t. Italian seasoning
salt and pepper to taste

26-oz. can favorite spaghetti
    sauce
6 to 8 slices provolone cheese

Cook pasta according to package directions; drain. Meanwhile, brown
beef in a skillet over medium heat; drain and stir in seasonings. Add
cooked pasta to a greased 3-quart casserole dish; stir in browned beef
and spaghetti sauce. Arrange cheese slices on top. Bake, uncovered, at
350 degrees for 25 to 30 minutes, until cheese is melted and bubbly.
Makes 6 to 8 servings.

Ranch-Style Beef & Bean Dinner

Leea Mercer
Edna, TX

This is a quick & easy recipe! Very yummy served with cornbread.

1 lb. ground beef
1/2 c. onion, chopped
salt and pepper to taste

2 15-oz. cans ranch-style beans
2 to 3 cloves garlic, minced

Brown beef and onion in a skillet over medium heat. Drain; season
with salt and pepper. Stir in beans and garlic; heat through. Makes
4 servings.

There is no need for hurry in life...
least of all when we are eating.
   – Edward Everett Hale

Italian Sausage Sandwiches

Karen Venable
Lakeland, FL

I remember when I was growing up, I'd visit a local restaurant that served these sandwiches. I can no longer get these sandwiches, so I came up with my own version to make at home and it's now a family favorite.

1-1/2 lbs. ground Italian
   pork sausage
4 hoagie rolls, split
Optional: softened butter, garlic
   powder to taste

1 sweet onion, thinly sliced
1 green, red or yellow sweet
   pepper, thinly sliced
16-oz. pkg. shredded Italian
   cheese, divided

Brown sausage in a skillet over medium heat; drain and set aside. If desired, brush cut sides of rolls with butter; sprinkle with garlic powder. Place bottoms of rolls in an ungreased 13"x9" baking pan. Top each with 1/2 cup cheese; top evenly with sausage, onion, pepper and remaining cheese. Add tops of rolls. Bake, uncovered, at 350 degrees for 5 to 10 minutes, until golden and cheese has melted. Makes 4 sandwiches.

Bacon Cheesy Hot Dogs

Denise Evans
Moosic, PA

Raising seven children, my mom figured out ways to serve a hot meal every night. This is a delicious, affordable recipe...my twist is the cheese over the bacon. Mom only used bacon. Either way, they are great. Serve with French fries.

8 to 10 hot dogs
8 to 10 thin slices bacon
8 to 10 slices Cooper or other
   favorite cheese, halved

8 to 10 hot dog rolls, split
   and warmed
Optional: catsup

Slice hot dogs down the center, but not all the way through. Place a bacon slice in the center of each hot dog; place on a broiler pan. Broil until bacon is almost browned. Remove from oven; top each slice of bacon with 2 half-slices of cheese. Broil for up to one minute, until cheese is melted. Place hot dogs in rolls; top with catsup, if desired. Serves 4 to 5, 2 hot dogs each.

FAMILY-PLEASING
Mains

Gobblin' Good Turkey Burgers

Brandi Glenn
Los Osos, CA

This was my mom's recipe...
I'll take these over plain old hamburgers any day!

1 lb. ground turkey
1 onion, minced
1 c. shredded Cheddar cheese
1/4 c. Worcestershire sauce

1/2 t. dry mustard
salt and pepper to taste
6 to 8 hamburger buns, split

Combine all ingredients except buns; form into 4 to 6 patties.
Grill to desired doneness; serve on hamburger buns. Makes
4 to 6 sandwiches.

When burgers and hot dogs are on the menu, set out a muffin tin filled
with shredded cheese, catsup or salsa, crispy bacon and other yummy
stuff. Everyone can just help themselves to their favorite toppings.

Barbecue Ham Sandwiches

Gloria Kaufmann
Orrville, OH

I often double this recipe...it reheats well and is always enjoyed by everyone. Serve on soft sandwich buns.

1 lb. deli chipped ham
1/2 c. catsup
1/2 c. onion, diced fine

1 t. vinegar
2 to 3 T. brown sugar, packed

Place ham in a lightly greased 2-quart casserole dish; set aside. Combine remaining ingredients in a small bowl; pour over ham and stir gently. Cover and bake at 300 degrees for one hour. Makes 6 sandwiches.

Pulled Pork Picnic Sandwiches

Nancy Kailihiwa
Wheatland, CA

Whenever life calls for a large gathering, I make this and always receive rave reviews. Wrap sandwiches in aluminum foil and place in an insulated pack or chest to keep warm.

3 to 6-lb. pork picnic or butt
  roast
1.1-oz. pkg. zesty ranch dip mix
1 onion, sliced and separated
  into rings

1/2 c. water
10 to 15 sweet French rolls,
  split

In a lightly greased skillet over medium heat, brown roast on all sides. Sprinkle dip mix over roast, turning to coat. Transfer to a greased 4 to 7-quart slow cooker, fat-side down. Top with onion rings. Pour water around roast, being careful not to rinse off dip mix. Cover and cook on high setting for one hour. Reduce setting to low; cook an additional 7 to 8 hours, until very tender. During the last hour, shred roast, discarding bones; return to slow cooker for the remaining time. Spoon shredded pork generously into rolls; spoon some of the juice onto the rolls. Makes 10 to 15 sandwiches.

Rolls and buns filled with juicy, slow-cooked meat will drip less if they're toasted first.

Shredded Buffalo Chicken Sliders

*Nola Coons
Gooseberry Patch*

These scrumptious mini sandwiches are always a hit at parties or get-togethers.

4 boneless, skinless chicken
   breasts
1/4 c. cayenne hot pepper sauce
2/3 c. water

16 dinner rolls, split
1 c. blue cheese salad dressing
Garnish: celery sticks

Place chicken breasts in a lightly greased slow cooker. In a bowl, stir together hot sauce and water; drizzle over chicken. Cover and cook on low setting for 8 hours. Remove chicken and shred with 2 forks; return to sauce in slow cooker. To serve, place shredded chicken on bottom halves of rolls; evenly top with dressing. Replace tops of rolls. Serve with celery sticks. Serves 8.

Super-Easy Italian Beef

*Deb Arch
Kewanee, IL*

While this recipe is cooking, your kitchen smells wonderful! It tastes like you worked all day making it, when all you did is put the two ingredients in the slow cooker! I like to serve this Italian beef on big soft hamburger buns and lots of mild jalapeño pepper slices.

2-lb. beef sirloin tip or
   rump roast

.6-oz. pkg. zesty Italian salad
   dressing mix

If desired, cut roast into 2-inch chunks to speed up cooking time. Place roast in a 4-quart slow cooker; sprinkle dressing mix over all. Do not add any water. Cover and cook on high setting for 2 hours. Turn to low setting for 6 hours, until roast is very tender and falling apart. Occasionally break up large pieces of roast with a large wooden spoon while cooking. Makes 8 sandwiches.

Paper coffee filters make tidy holders for tacos and sandwiches.

Dad's Chicken & Noodles

Terisa Vest
New Albany, IN

My dad first fixed this one Sunday when my four sisters,
my brother and I were kids. We loved this so much,
Mom would tell Daddy, it's time for chicken & noodles!

3 lbs. chicken
2 to 3 cubes chicken bouillon
14-oz. can chicken broth
16-oz. pkg. wide egg noodles,
  uncooked

23-oz. can cream of chicken
  soup

Cover chicken with water in a stockpot; add bouillon cubes. Bring to
a boil over high heat. Reduce heat to low; cover and simmer for
45 minutes to one hour, until no longer pink. Remove chicken to a
bowl and cool, reserving broth in pot. Shred chicken and return to
broth in pot. Add canned broth; bring to a boil. Stir in uncooked egg
noodles and cook until tender, about 20 minutes. Stir in soup and
simmer about 10 minutes more. Makes 6 to 7 servings.

Lip-Smackin' Chicken & Gravy

Pat Beach
Fisherville, KY

My family loves this super-easy and oh-so-yummy slow-cooker dish.
The gravy is fabulous served over mashed potatoes.

6 boneless, skinless chicken
  breasts
2 10-3/4 oz. cans cream of
  chicken soup

10-3/4 oz. can cream of
  mushroom soup

Place chicken breasts in a 6-quart slow cooker. Mix soups together in
a bowl. Spread soup mixture over chicken. Cover and cook on low
setting for 8 hours, or until chicken is fork-tender. Makes 6 servings.

No cream of mushroom soup in the pantry? Cream of celery or
chicken is sure to be just as tasty...you may even discover
a new way you like even better!

FAMILY-PLEASING
Mains

Quick-as-a-Wink Chicken & Dumplin's

Tracie Carlson
Richardson, TX

An excellent quick remedy for cold sufferers...just add lots of freshly minced garlic!

8 c. chicken broth or water
2 T. chicken bouillon granules
4 to 6 cloves garlic, minced
1 lb. boneless, skinless chicken
    breast tenders

16-oz. tube refrigerated flaky
    biscuits
Garnish: dried parsley

Bring broth or water to a boil in a stockpot over high heat; add bouillon and garlic. Reduce heat to medium; add chicken tenders. Simmer for 10 minutes. Separate biscuits and tear each biscuit into 3 or 4 pieces. Drop biscuit pieces into simmering broth mixture; reduce heat to low. Continue cooking at a low simmer for another 15 to 20 minutes, until chicken and biscuit pieces are cooked through. Sprinkle with parsley before serving. Makes 6 servings.

For another way to make tasty dumplings, mix up 2 cups biscuit baking mix with 3/4 cup milk. You can even add a teaspoon of snipped parsley or thyme. Drop large spoonfuls of batter into simmering soup. Cover and cook for about 15 minutes, until dumplings are set.

3-Ingredient Turkey Pie

Angela Bissette
Middlesex, NC

This is a recipe I created when I wanted a quick and delicious holiday meal. Serve with green beans, rolls and cranberry sauce for a complete meal.

6-oz. pkg. chicken-flavored
   stuffing mix

2 c. cooked turkey, diced
12-oz. jar turkey gravy

Prepare stuffing mix according to directions. Press half of stuffing into a 9" glass pie plate. Bake at 350 degrees for 10 minutes. Mix together turkey and gravy; spoon into baked crust. Add remaining stuffing on top. Bake at 350 degrees for 15 to 20 minutes, until hot and bubbly. Serves 6.

Easy Chicken Pot Pie

Ellie Brandel
Clackamas, OR

Cooked turkey and even beef are good in this recipe too. A great way to serve up leftovers!

2 9-inch refrigerated pie crusts
10-oz. pkg. frozen mixed
   vegetables
1 c. water

10-3/4 oz. can cream of
   mushroom, chicken or
   celery soup
2 c. cooked chicken, cubed

Unfold one crust and arrange in a 9" pie plate or round casserole dish; set aside. Combine frozen vegetables and water in a saucepan. Bring to a boil over medium-high heat. Boil for one minute; drain. In a bowl, combine vegetables, soup and chicken; spoon mixture into pie crust. Add remaining crust on top; seal. Cut several vents in top crust with a knife tip. Bake at 350 degrees for 30 to 40 minutes, until bubbly and golden. Serves 4.

Cut vents in your pot pie crust with a chicken-shaped mini cookie cutter... so sweet.

FAMILY-PLEASING
Mains

Mother's Turkey Divan

Wendi Smith
Zanesville, OH

*This recipe belonged to my mother and everyone loves it.
It's affordable, easy and very delicious.*

3 c. broccoli, cut into bite-size
  flowerets
6 slices deli smoked turkey
  breast, 1/4-inch thick

6 slices Swiss cheese
18-oz. jar turkey gravy
salt and pepper to taste

In a saucepan, cover broccoli with water. Bring to a boil over high heat; cook until almost tender, about 6 minutes. Drain well and set aside. Lay out one slice of turkey on a flat surface; add one slice of Swiss cheese to the center, then arrange several broccoli flowerets across cheese. Roll up turkey slice, starting at one end and being careful that all ingredients stay in roll. Repeat until all ingredients are used. Arrange turkey rolls in a lightly greased shallow 13"x9" baking pan. Spoon gravy over rolls. Cover and bake at 375 degrees for 30 minutes, or until hot and bubbly. Makes 6 servings.

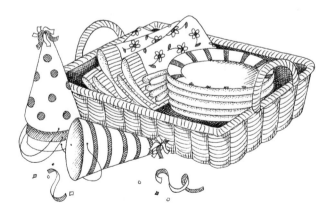

Keep some festive paper plates and napkins tucked away...
they'll set a lighthearted mood on busy evenings,
with easy clean-up afterwards.

Pork & Sweet Potatoes

Nancy Wise
Little Rock, AR

Sweet and fruity...a slow-cooker holiday meal in one!

15-oz. jar sweetened applesauce
3 lbs. sweet potatoes, peeled
   and sliced
1/4 c. brown sugar, packed
3/4 t. salt, divided

1/4 t. pepper, divided
6 6-oz. bone-in pork loin chops
14-oz. can whole-berry
   cranberry sauce

Spoon applesauce into a 6-quart slow cooker. Arrange sweet potato slices on top. Sprinkle with brown sugar, 1/4 teaspoon salt and 1/8 teaspoon pepper. Arrange pork chops over sweet potatoes; sprinkle with remaining salt and pepper. Spoon cranberry sauce over pork. Cover and cook on low setting for 6 to 8 hours, until pork and sweet potatoes are tender. Makes 6 servings.

Oh-so-easy iced tea...perfect with dinner anytime. Fill a 2-quart pitcher with water and drop in 6 to 8 tea bags. Refrigerate for several hours. Discard tea bags; add sugar to taste and serve over ice.

Golden Parmesan Roasted Potatoes, page 63

Pantry Tomato Soup, page 15

Marinated Flank Steak, page 96

Poppy Seed Chicken, page 102

Gobblin' Good Turkey Burgers, page 119

Chicken & Rice Casserole, page 104

Chili-Weather Chili, page 38

Hot Bacon-Potato Salad, page 57

Butter Pecan Peach Cake, page 183

Southwestern Flatbread, page 22

Hawaiian Meatballs, page 173

Loaded Potato Soup, page 33

Shredded Buffalo Chicken Sliders, page 121

Dilly Cucumber Salad, page 59

Spinach Casserole, page 69

Tempting Teriyaki Chicken, page 88

Jalapeño Popper Pinwheels, page 148

Cherry-Pineapple Dump Cake, page 215

Melinda's Veggie Stir-Fry, page 116

Lizzy's Make-Ahead Egg Casserole, page 129

Maple Pork Chops, page 91

Texas Queso Dip, page 164

Speedy Peanut Butter Cookies, page 180

FAMILY-PLEASING
Mains

So-Easy BBQ Pork Ribs

Rose Fern
Newport, NC

All the kids look forward to getting this slow-cooker meal when they come back home. Serve over steamed rice, with corn on the cob and a side of coleslaw...homemade ice cream for dessert. Wonderful! Any leftovers are great on hamburger buns.

4 to 6 lbs. boneless country-
    style pork ribs, cut into
    serving-size pieces

18-oz. bottle favorite barbecue
    sauce
1/4 to 1/2 c. water

Place ribs in a 5 to 6-quart slow cooker. Cover ribs with barbecue sauce. Add 1/4 cup water for 4 pounds of ribs, up to 1/2 cup water for 6 pounds. Cover and cook on low setting for 8 to 10 hours. Makes 6 to 8 servings.

Best Slow-Cooked Pork Ribs

Barbara Cebula
Chicopee, MA

I fix these ribs on days that I am in a rush for a great and hearty meal. Serve coleslaw on the side...yummy!

4 lbs. boneless country-style
    pork ribs, cut into serving-
    size pieces
1 c. barbecue sauce

1 c. Catalina salad dressing
1/2 t. garlic, minced
2 T. all-purpose flour
1/2 c. cold water

Arrange ribs in a 5-quart slow cooker. Combine barbecue sauce and salad dressing; spoon over ribs. Sprinkle with garlic. Cover and cook on low setting for 6 to 7 hours, until tender. Remove ribs to a platter; cover to keep warm. Strain cooking liquid into a small saucepan and skim fat. Stir together flour and water until smooth; stir into cooking liquid. Bring to a boil; cook and stir for 2 minutes, until thickened. Serve sauce with ribs. Makes 8 servings.

Jazz up a packaged wild rice mix in a jiffy. Sauté a cup of chopped mushrooms, onion and celery in butter until tender, then add rice mix and prepare as usual.

Cornbread Sausage Casserole

Kathy Grashoff
Fort Wayne, IN

Something different to serve for brunch...or even for dinner!

1 lb. ground pork sausage
16-oz. pkg. cornbread mix
15-oz. can cream-style corn
1/2 c. plus 2 T. water
3/4 c. onion, diced

Optional: 4 diced jalapeño
   peppers, or to taste
2 c. shredded Cheddar-Monterey
   Jack cheese

Brown sausage in a skillet over medium heat; drain and set aside.
Combine cornbread mix, corn and water in a bowl; spread a 1/2-inch
layer of batter in a greased 11"x7" baking pan. Layer sausage, onion,
jalapeño if using and cheese over batter. Top with remaining batter.
Bake, uncovered, at 350 degrees for 35 minutes. Let stand 10 minutes
before serving. Serves 8.

Biscuits & Gravy Casserole

Sarah Slaven
Strunk, KY

*My husband's favorite dish is biscuits & gravy. This is an easy and
tasty way to make his day, no matter what time of day it's served.*

1 lb. ground pork sausage
2 8-oz. tubes refrigerated
   biscuits, quartered
4 to 5 eggs

1/2 c. milk
salt and pepper to taste
2-oz. pkg. country gravy mix

Brown sausage in a skillet over medium heat; drain. Arrange biscuit
pieces in a lightly greased 13"x9" baking pan. Layer sausage over
biscuits, reserving drippings and 1/4 cup sausage. Beat eggs with milk;
season with salt and pepper and pour over sausage. Prepare gravy
according to package directions, adding reserved sausage and
drippings; spoon over egg mixture. Cover and bake at 350 degrees
for about one hour. Makes 6 servings.

No time for a leisurely family breakfast? Try serving breakfast
for dinner...it's sure to become a family favorite!

Lizzy's Make-Ahead Egg Casserole

Lizzy Burnley
Ankeny, IA

This recipe is a favorite for breakfast, lunch or dinner. And preparing it ahead makes it that much easier! It is perfect for serving after the Easter egg hunt or for a Mother's Day brunch.

1 doz. eggs, beaten
1 c. cooked ham, diced
3 c. whole milk

12 frozen waffles, divided
2 c. shredded Cheddar cheese, divided

In a large bowl, beat eggs. Stir in ham and milk. Grease a 13"x9" baking pan. Place one layer of waffles in the bottom of the pan. Pour half of the mixture on the waffles. Sprinkle with half of the cheese. Continue layering waffles, egg mixture and cheese. Cover and refrigerate overnight. Uncover and bake at 350 degrees for about one hour, until eggs are set. Serves 12.

Surprisingly, canned tomatoes actually have even more health benefits than fresh tomatoes. With a few cans of already-seasoned tomatoes in the pantry, you can whip up a flavorful meal anytime.

Reuben Brunch Casserole

Leona Krivda
Belle Vernon, PA

We like breakfast anytime, so I make this dish for dinner once in awhile too. Put it together in the morning, serve that night.

10 slices rye bread, cut into
    3/4-inch cubes
1-1/2 lbs. cooked corned beef,
    coarsely shredded
10-oz. pkg. Swiss cheese,
    shredded

6 eggs, lightly beaten
3 c. milk
1/4 t. pepper

Arrange bread cubes in a greased 13"x9" baking pan. Layer corned beef over bread cubes; sprinkle with cheese. In a bowl, beat together eggs, milk and pepper; pour over top. Cover with aluminum foil and refrigerate for 8 hours to overnight. Bake, covered, at 350 degrees for 45 minutes. Uncover and bake an additional 10 minutes. Serve immediately. Makes 6 to 8 servings.

Chicken Reuben

Amy Hunt
Traphill, NC

Not your ordinary baked chicken, but it's so tasty! Maybe even a new favorite at your dinner table.

4 boneless, skinless chicken
    breasts
14-oz. can sauerkraut, drained

4 slices Swiss cheese
1-1/4 c. Thousand Island salad
    dressing

Spray a 13"x9" baking pan with non-stick vegetable spray; arrange chicken in pan. Spread sauerkraut evenly over chicken; top with cheese. Spoon salad dressing over cheese. Cover with aluminum foil. Bake at 325 degrees for 1-1/2 hours. Makes 4 servings.

Boneless chicken breasts cook up quickly and evenly when flattened between 2 pieces of plastic wrap with a meat mallet.

Creamy Sloppy Joes

Jenita Davison
La Plata, MO

My mom, who didn't especially care for tomato-based Sloppy Joes, shared this recipe with me many years ago. It's a nice change of pace and great comfort food. Spoon onto buns or over slices of toast.

1-1/2 lbs. ground beef
Optional: 1/4 c. onion, diced
10-3/4 oz. can cream of
   mushroom soup

2 T. Worcestershire sauce
1/4 c. catsup
1/3 c. light brown sugar, packed

In a large skillet over medium heat, brown beef with onion, if using; drain. Stir in remaining ingredients. Reduce heat to medium-low. Simmer until flavors are blended, about 10 minutes. Makes 4 servings.

Laughter really is the best medicine! Studies show that time spent laughing provides all kinds of health benefits...it can even burn extra calories. So be sure to share funny stories and the kids' latest jokes everyday over dinner.

Quinoa Stuffed Peppers

Joni Rick
Hemet, CA

Looking for a way to make stuffed peppers with a healthy dairy-free vegetarian twist, I came up with this tasty blend of flavors. It's easy to fix in a slow cooker. To make this dish kid-friendly, drizzle peppers with your favorite barbecue sauce before serving.

2-1/4 c. water, divided
1 t. salt
1 c. quinoa, uncooked
4-oz. can mushroom pieces,
   drained

15-oz. can corn, drained
15-oz. can black beans, drained
   and rinsed
8 green peppers, tops removed

In a large saucepan over medium-high heat, bring 2 cups water to a boil. Stir in quinoa and salt. Reduce heat to medium-low. Cover and simmer for 12 to 15 minutes, until all liquid is absorbed. Combine cooked quinoa, mushrooms, corn and beans. Spoon mixture into peppers; arrange in a 6-quart slow cooker. Add remaining water to bottom of slow cooker. Cover and cook on low setting for 4 to 5 hours, until peppers are tender. Makes 8 servings.

Easy Pizza Peppers

Nicole Wood
Ontario, Canada

This recipe is also great with Cheddar cheese. Try adding olives, pineapple tidbits or your favorite pizza toppings too!

1 lb. extra lean ground beef
1/2 c. onion, chopped
salt and pepper to taste
4 red or yellow peppers, halved
   lengthwise

4 T. water, divided
15-oz. bottle pizza sauce
Garnish: shredded mozzarella
   cheese

Brown beef with onion, salt and pepper in a skillet over medium heat; drain. Place pepper halves on 2 plates; add 2 tablespoons water to each plate. Microwave on high for 5 minutes, or until peppers are soft. Spoon beef mixture into peppers; arrange on a baking sheet. Spoon pizza sauce onto beef mixture; cover with cheese. Bake at 375 degrees for 15 minutes, or until cheese is melted. Makes 4 servings.

Busy Mom's Biscuit Cheeseburger Pizza

Rachel Rowden
Festus, MO

This is a go-to for my family of four on those nights we have softball and tee ball practice. My 12-year-old daughter Isabella and 6-year-old daughter Carly both love this recipe.

1 lb ground beef
1 T. dried minced onion
salt and pepper to taste
10-3/4 oz. can Cheddar
   cheese soup

16-oz. tube refrigerated biscuits
1 c. shredded Cheddar cheese
Garnish: cheeseburger
   condiments

Brown beef in a skillet with onion; drain and season with salt and pepper. Stir in soup; set aside. Stretch biscuits and press together to form a crust; place on a baking sheet sprayed with non-stick vegetable spray. Top crust with beef mixture; sprinkle evenly with cheese. Bake at 350 degrees for 10 minutes, or until crust is golden and cheese is melted. Cut into squares; serve with your favorite condiments. Makes 8 servings.

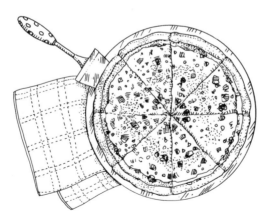

For a brand-new meal your family will love, pizza-fy those leftovers! Top a ready-to-bake crust with pizza sauce, sliced baked chicken or grilled steak, veggies and whatever sounds good to you. Finish with a sprinkle of cheese and bake until hot and bubbly, about 10 minutes at 400 degrees. Yummy!

Eggplant Mexicana

Dayle Hodakievic
Willoughby, OH

Even kids will like this one! The recipe came about when I was pressed for time and had some frozen taco beef and a large eggplant on hand. It was a success!

1 lb. lean ground beef
1-1/4 oz. pkg. taco seasoning
  mix
2/3 c. water
1-1/2 c. shredded Cheddar
  cheese

1 large eggplant, peeled and
  sliced lengthwise, 1/2-inch
  thick
Italian salad dressing to taste

Brown beef in a skillet over medium heat; drain. Stir in taco seasoning and water. Bring to a boil; simmer for 3 to 4 minutes. Keep warm. Coat both sides of eggplant slices with salad dressing; arrange on a broiler pan. Broil eggplant until tender and golden on both sides. Top each slice with beef mixture and cheese. Broil for another 2 minutes, or until cheese is melted. Makes 4 to 6 servings.

Potato Tot Casserole

Michele Shenk
Manheim, PA

I first made this casserole when my children were younger. The potato puffs were a big hit, and still are! It's easy to prepare and goes well with a crisp side salad.

1 lb. ground beef
1/2 c. onion, chopped
10-3/4 oz. can cream of chicken
  or celery soup

10-oz. pkg. frozen peas
32-oz. pkg. frozen potato puffs,
  divided

Press uncooked beef into a lightly greased 8"x8" baking pan. Layer with onion, soup and frozen peas. Top with half of frozen potato puffs; return the rest to the freezer for another recipe. Bake, uncovered, at 350 degrees for about one hour. Serves 4 to 5.

SPEEDY
Snacks & Appetizers

Chicken-Pesto Pinwheels

Lori Ritchey
Denver, PA

These pinwheels are perfect for a snack or light lunch. You can swap chicken for turkey and use spinach or tomato tortillas for the plain ones too. A great appetizer before an Italian meal!

8-oz. pkg. cream cheese,
  softened
6-oz. jar pesto sauce
1/2 c. shredded Parmesan
  cheese

Optional: finely sliced sun-dried
  tomatoes to taste
6 10-inch flour tortillas
1 lb. sliced deli roast chicken

In a bowl, blend cream cheese, pesto, Parmesan cheese and tomatoes, if using. Spread mixture evenly on tortillas; arrange chicken slices over cheese spread. Roll up each tortilla jelly-roll style and press edges to seal. Wrap each roll in plastic wrap to seal. Keep refrigerated until ready to serve. To serve, slice each roll into 6 pieces on the diagonal. Makes 3 dozen.

Here's a tip for any buffet table...stack your plates at the beginning, but save the silverware, napkins and beverages for the end of the line. So much easier to handle!

SPEEDY Snacks & Appetizers

Mini Chicken Caesar Cups

Mia Rossi
Charlotte, NC

Tasty little morsels that my guests love! I like to prep the filling and press the biscuits into the muffin tin a bit ahead of time. Then it's a snap to bake and fill at party time.

12-oz. tube refrigerated
 flaky biscuits
1 c. cooked chicken, finely
 chopped
3 T. Caesar salad dressing

1/4 c. romaine lettuce, finely
 sliced
1/4 c. shredded Parmesan
 cheese

Separate biscuits; split each biscuit into 2 layers. Press biscuit pieces into 20 ungreased mini muffin cups; dough should extend 1/4 inch above cups. In a small bowl, mix chicken and dressing. Spoon 2 teaspoons of mixture into each cup. Bake at 400 degrees for 8 to 11 minutes, until crust is deeply golden. Remove from muffin tin; top with lettuce and cheese. Serve warm. Makes 20 pieces.

Victorian Iced Tea

Janis Parr
Ontario, Canada

This crisp, refreshing drink is a welcome change from the sweeter fruit punches usually served in the hot summertime. You may substitute different fruit juices to suit your taste.

4 c. boiling water
4 tea bags
12-oz. can frozen citrus-blend
 juice concentrate, thawed

4 c. cold water
Garnish: orange and lemon
 slices

Pour boiling water into a teapot. Add tea bags and cover; steep for 5 minutes. Discard tea bags. Chill tea in a covered container. Just before serving, combine citrus juice and cold water in a 3-quart pitcher; stir in tea. Add orange and lemon slices; serve over ice. Makes 10 servings.

Freeze ice cubes from orange juice. Not only do they garnish the drink, they add more flavor as they melt.

Avocado Salsa

Paulette Walters
Newfoundland, Canada

I love to make this appetizer whenever I have
a girls' night in! It's tasty with tortilla chips.

1 avocado, peeled, pitted
   and diced
1 tomato, diced
1 T. red onion, minced

2 t. extra virgin olive oil
2 t. lemon juice
1/8 t. salt
1/8 t. pepper

Combine all ingredients in a bowl; mix well. Cover and refrigerate if
preparing in advance. Bring to room temperature before serving.
Serves 4 to 6.

Bean & Roasted Garlic Dip
Lisa Ann Panzino DiNunzio
Vineland, NJ

This dip is delicious...perfect to serve at gatherings and parties!
Serve with toasted semolina, French or multi-grain bread,
crackers or a veggie tray.

15-oz. can cannellini beans,
   drained and rinsed
6 cloves garlic, roasted

2 T. extra virgin olive oil
2 T. lemon juice
sea salt and pepper to taste

Combine all ingredients in a blender or food processor. Blend until
smooth. Chill until serving time. Serves 6.

Roasted garlic is delicious in recipes...wonderful spread on
French bread. Cut off the top of a garlic bulb, exposing the cloves.
Brush generously with olive oil and place in a lightly oiled small
casserole dish. Bake, uncovered, at 350 degrees for about
35 minutes, until pulp is very soft.

Mexican Dip

Shanna Hunt
Penhook, VA

*This recipe is so simple and quick. It is a family favorite for any
get-together, game day or holiday. Serve with tortilla chips.*

16-oz. can refried beans
8-oz. container sour cream
4-1/2 oz. can diced green chiles
1-oz. pkg ranch dip mix

16-oz. pkg. shredded Mexican-
blend cheese, divided
Optional: sliced green onions,
cherry tomatoes, black olives

In a microwave-safe bowl, combine beans, sour cream, chiles, dip mix
and 2 cups cheese. Microwave on high for 2 minutes; stir. Microwave
2 more minutes; stir until well blended and cheese is melted. Transfer
to a serving bowl; top with remaining cheese. Serve warm, garnished
as desired. Serves 10 to 12.

The secret to being a relaxed hostess...choose foods that can be
prepared in advance. At party time, simply pull from the fridge
and serve, or pop into a hot oven as needed.

Tipsy Meatballs

Pearl Teiserskas
Brookfield, IL

Our family was always getting together for the holidays. Family would travel from all over the country to celebrate Memorial Day in our hometown of Ocean City, Maryland. This was one of our favorite appetizers to start off our meals.

3 lbs. ground beef
1 onion, grated
salt and pepper to taste
14-oz. bottle catsup

20-oz. can regular or
   non-alcoholic beer
1/4 c. water

Combine beef, onion, salt and pepper in a large bowl; mix well. Form into bite-size meatballs and set aside. In a large saucepan, combine catsup, beer and water; heat through over medium-low heat. Carefully add meatballs to hot sauce. Reduce heat to low. Simmer for one hour, stirring occasionally. Transfer meatballs with sauce to a chafing dish or slow cooker; serve warm. Makes about 4 dozen.

Peppery Buttermilk Wings

Nola Coons
Gooseberry Patch

You'll score a touchdown at your next tailgate party with this flavorful two-ingredient recipe.

2-1/2 lbs. chicken wings,
   separated

1.15-oz. pkg. peppered country
   gravy mix

Place chicken wings in a large bowl; sprinkle with gravy mix and toss to coat. Spray an aluminum foil-lined 15"x10" jelly-roll pan with non-stick vegetable spray. Arrange wings on pan in a single layer. Bake at 450 degrees for 30 to 35 minutes, until crisp, golden and chicken juices run clear. Serves 8.

For stand-up parties, do your guests a favor by serving foods
that can be eaten in just one or 2 bites.

Cathy's BLT Dip

Cathy Miller
Benton, AR

I make this dip every year for Thanksgiving and it goes so fast! It is good with crackers, sliced French bread, party rye bread or veggies.

2 8-oz. pkgs. cream cheese,
   softened
1 c. mayonnaise
1/2 c. sour cream

14-1/2 oz. can petite diced
   tomatoes, well drained
1/2 lb. bacon, crisply cooked
   and crumbled

Place cream cheese in a large bowl; stir with a fork until creamy. Add mayonnaise and sour cream; mix well. Carefully fold in tomatoes and 3/4 of bacon. Transfer to a serving bowl; top with remaining bacon. Serves 12 to 15.

Bacon & Apricot Bites

Jill Ball
Highland, UT

Warning...this appetizer with disappear before your eyes! One minute you have a full plate and the next they're gone! My husband once topped them with blue cheese and they were out of this world. A great little appetizer for parties.

24 dried apricots
12 slices bacon, halved

3/4 c. brown sugar, packed

Wrap each apricot in a half-slice of bacon; secure with a toothpick. Roll in brown sugar; arrange on a lightly greased baking sheet. Bake at 350 degrees for about 20 minutes, until bacon is crisp. Makes 2 dozen.

Need to soften cream cheese in a hurry? Simply place an unwrapped 8-ounce block on a plate and microwave for about a minute at 50% power.

Party Ham Pinwheels

Gladys Kielar
Whitehouse, OH

*Shower parties and graduations always bring out
these family appetizers. Easy to make and so tasty!*

4 thin slices deli boiled ham
8-oz. pkg. cream cheese,
   softened and divided

4 t. fresh chives, chopped
   and divided
40 round buttery crackers

Spread each ham slice with 1/4 cup cream cheese, spreading to the edges. Sprinkle each with one teaspoon chives. Beginning at one short end, roll up tightly. Wrap individually in plastic wrap. refrigerate for at least 2 hours. At serving time, slice each roll crosswise into 10 slices. Place one slice on each cracker. Serve immediately. Makes 40 pieces.

Festive trimmings can turn the simplest fare into a feast.
Pick up some brightly colored napkins and table coverings at
the nearest dollar store and you're halfway to a party!

Beef Pinwheel Appetizers

Diana Chaney
Olathe, KS

Easy to make...scrumptious to eat!

8-oz. pkg. cream cheese,
  softened
1 T. onion, grated

1 t. creamy horseradish sauce
1/4 t. Worcestershire sauce
2 2-oz. pkgs. sliced dried beef

In a bowl, blend cream cheese, onion and sauces well. Lay out beef slices, slightly overlapping 2 slices in a row. Spread with cream cheese mixture; roll up and fasten with a toothpick. Repeat with remaining ingredients. Cover and refrigerate at least 2 hours. Just before serving, cut into one-inch slices. Serves 10.

Dill Pickle Wraps

Jennifer Tennyson
Boonville, IN

Good for Sunday afternoon game days.

32-oz. jar dill pickle spears,
  drained
1 lb. thinly sliced deli baked
  ham

8-oz. pkg. cream cheese,
  softened

Drain pickles on paper towels; pat dry. Spread each ham slice with 2 tablespoons cream cheese; lay a pickle spear on top and roll up. Cover and refrigerate at least one hour. Slice rolls into bite-size chunks; fasten with toothpicks. Makes 15 to 20 servings.

A multitude of small delights constitutes happiness.
– Charles Baudelaire

Taste of Italy Spread

Karyn Woods
Stanhope, NJ

This easy recipe is always requested whenever we go to parties. It also a family staple at our Christmas Eve dinner. Not only is it easy to make, but it tastes and looks great. Serve with slices of baguette bread or snack crackers.

8-oz. pkg. cream cheese,
    softened
2 T. sour cream
1/2 c. black olives, chopped

1/2 c. sun-dried tomatoes,
    finely chopped
1/4 c. red onion, finely chopped

In a bowl, mix cream cheese and sour cream until well blended. Add remaining ingredients; gently mix well. Cover and chill until serving time. Serves 12.

Carolyn's Slush Punch

Carolyn Gochenaur
Howe, IN

There's nothing like a cold, slushy drink on a hot summer day. Choose your favorite gelatin fruit flavor. Cheers!

6-oz. pkg cherry gelatin mix
4 c. boiling water
8 c. cold water

14-oz. can pineapple juice
1-1/2 c. sugar
2 ltrs. lemon-lime soda, chilled

In a large heatproof container, dissolve gelatin mix in boiling water. Stir in remaining ingredients except soda. Cover and freeze for 24 hours. To serve, let stand at room temperature for 15 to 30 minutes. Transfer to a punch bowl; chop into small chunks. Pour desired amount of soda over slush. Makes 16 servings.

Dress up glasses of lemonade or iced tea by dipping the rims into lemon juice, then into sparkling sugar.

SPEEDY **Snacks & Appetizers**

Cheesy Bruschetta

Scarlett Hedden
Titusville, FL

Oh yum...this simple little recipe is so darn good!
Easy to make and great for football parties or when
you need a deelish appetizer.

1/2 c. grated Parmesan cheese
1/4 c. red onion or green onions,
   finely chopped

1/2 c. mayonnaise
1 long thin French loaf, sliced
   1/4 to 1/2-inch thick

Combine cheese, onion and mayonnaise in a small bowl; mix well.
Spread one tablespoon of mixture on each bread slice; cut each slice in
half. Arrange on ungreased baking sheets. Bake at 350 degrees until
bubbly and golden, about 8 to 10 minutes, watching closely to avoid
burning. Makes 12 to 15 servings.

Tasty Pizza Sticks

Tracy Stoll
Seville, OH

An easy snack kids can help make, then enjoy.

11-oz. tube refrigerated
   bread sticks
24 slices pepperoni
2 T. grated Parmesan cheese

1/2 t. Italian seasoning
1/4 t. garlic powder
Garnish: warmed pizza sauce

Separate and unroll bread sticks. On one half of each bread stick, place
3 slices of pepperoni. Fold remaining half over top. Seal and twist.
Place on an ungreased baking sheet. In a cup, combine cheese and
seasonings; sprinkle evenly over bread sticks. Bake at 350 degrees for
15 to 20 minutes, until golden. Serve with pizza sauce for dipping.
Makes 8 servings.

Roquefort Dip

Susan Schmirler
Hartland, WI

This recipe was originally served at the bar of one of our favorite Wisconsin restaurants. We loved it so much that we have since adopted it as one of our family favorites that we enjoy during the holidays. Serve with ruffled potato chips or snack crackers.

2 cubes beef bouillon
1 T. hot water
8-oz. pkg. cream cheese,
    softened
3 T. sour cream

minced onion to taste
3 T. crumbled Roquefort cheese,
    or more to taste
Optional: half-and-half to taste

Combine bouillon cubes and hot water in a cup; let stand until dissolved. In a large bowl, combine bouillon, cream cheese, sour cream and onion. Beat with an electric mixer on medium speed until fluffy. Stir in Roquefort cheese. If necessary, stir in a little half-and-half to thin dip to a thinner consistency. Cover and chill until serving time. Serves 6 to 8.

Make a party tray of savory bite-size appetizer tarts...guests will never suspect how easy it is! Bake frozen mini phyllo shells according to package directions, then spoon in a favorite creamy dip or spread.

SPEEDY **Snacks & Appetizers**

Yummy Reuben Dip

Judy Lange
Imperial, PA

Yummy, fast and gone in no time...might have to double it!

2 8-oz. pkgs. cream cheese,
  softened
8-oz. container sour cream
3 2-oz. pkgs. sliced dried
  corned beef, chopped

8-oz. can sauerkraut, drained
6-oz. pkg. shredded Swiss
  cheese
cocktail rye bread or rye crackers

Combine all ingredients in a 3-quart slow cooker. Cover and cook on
low setting for about 3 hours; stir to blend. Serve hot with bread or
crackers. Makes 10 to 12 servings.

Beer Cheese Dip

Diana Krol
Nickerson, KS

This is the perfect game-day dip...everyone just stands around
the bowl and chows down! Serve with your favorite
pretzels or pretzel-style crackers.

2 8-oz. pkgs. cream cheese,
  softened
8-oz. pkg. shredded Cheddar
  cheese

1 c. regular or non-alcoholic beer
1-oz. pkg. ranch salad dressing
  mix

In a large bowl, beat together all ingredients until light and fluffy.
Cover and refrigerate for several hours to overnight. Makes 5 cups.

Try red pepper strips, endive
leaves, cucumber slices and
snow peas as fresh and tasty
alternatives to chips for
scooping up creamy dips.

Jalapeño Popper Pinwheels

Jessica Kraus
Delaware, OH

This is such a great recipe for football season!

4-oz. can diced jalapeño
  peppers, drained
8-oz. pkg. cream cheese,
  softened
1 c. shredded Mexican-blend
  cheese

2 t. salt
8-oz. tube refrigerated crescent
  rolls
grated Parmesan cheese
  to taste

In a large bowl, combine jalapeños, cheeses and salt; blend well and
set aside. Unroll crescent rolls; seal seams but do not separate. Spread
cream cheese mixture evenly over the dough. Roll up jelly-roll style;
slice the roll into 1/3-inch slices. Arrange on a lightly greased baking
sheet, leaving one inch between slices. Dust with Parmesan cheese.
Bake at 375 degrees for 11 to 15 minutes, until tops begin to turn
golden. Let cool for a minute, then transfer to a cooling rack. Makes 8.

Stuffed Jalapeños

Carla Whitfield
Bonham, TX

*I wanted to make stuffed jalapeños for my husband. I had never
made them before and he always enjoyed them when other people
made them. So I came up with this...he loves them!*

10 large jalapeño peppers
1-1/2 c. shredded Cheddar
  cheese
2 12-oz. cans chicken, partially
  drained

1-1/4 oz. pkg. taco seasoning
  mix
10 slices bacon

Cut each jalapeño pepper across the top; cut a slit and open up pepper.
Remove seeds and membranes; set aside. In a bowl, combine cheese,
chicken and taco seasoning; mix well. Stuff peppers with mixture.
Wrap each with a bacon slice; use a wooden toothpick to fasten.
Place peppers on an ungreased baking sheet. Bake at 325 degrees for
40 to 45 minutes, until peppers are soft and bacon is chewy. Makes
10 servings.

SPEEDY Snacks & Appetizers

Marla's Good Salsa

Marla Kinnersley
Surprise, AZ

A favorite in our home...there's just something about this salsa that keeps everyone coming back for more. We really enjoy it with lime-flavored tortilla chips!

28-oz. can crushed tomatoes
3 T. fresh cilantro, chopped
2 t. canned pickled jalapeño
   peppers, minced

1/2 t. garlic powder
1/2 t. ground cumin
1/4 t. salt

In a serving bowl, combine tomatoes with juice and remaining ingredients; mix well. Cover and chill for at least one hour before serving. Serves 4.

Family night! Make some favorite snacks and spend the evening playing favorite board games together.

Chicken Salad Cucumber Bites

Courtney Stultz
Weir, KS

These chicken salad bites are perfect. They are light, healthy and crisp, making a great lunch, snack or appetizer! Use your favorite light mayonnaise for an even healthier option.

1 c. cooked chicken, shredded
1/4 c. seedless grapes, chopped
1/4 c. mayonnaise
1/2 t. dill weed

1/4 t. sea salt
1/4 t. pepper
1 cucumber, peeled and
   sliced 1/4-inch thick

In a bowl, combine all ingredients except cucumber; mix well. Scoop into spoonfuls and place on cucumber slices. Serves 2 to 4.

Alan's Almond Tea Punch

Ramona Wysong
Barlow, KY

This is a recipe my late husband Alan loved to make... something a little different for parties.

4 c. boiling water
4 tea bags
6-oz. can frozen lemonade
   concentrate, thawed

3 c. cold water
1/2 c. sugar, or to taste
1/2 t. almond extract

In a heatproof pitcher, combine boiling water and tea bags. Steep to desired strength; discard tea bags. Add remaining ingredients; stir well to dissolve sugar. Cover and chill; serve over ice. Makes 16 small servings.

The next time a party guest asks, "How can I help?" be ready with an answer! Whether it's picking up a bag of ice, setting the table or even bringing a special dessert, friends are usually happy to lend a hand.

SPEEDY Snacks & Appetizers

Pineapple-Ham Crescents

Marsha Baker
Pioneer, OH

I found this delectable recipe in my mom's files after she had passed away. It has become a favorite, for more reasons than one. She used canned pineapple spears, which aren't easy to find anymore, but pineapple chunks work well.

8-oz. tube refrigerated
    crescent rolls
8 thin slices deli ham,
    2 inches wide
8 slices Swiss cheese,
    2 inches wide

20-oz. can pineapple chunks
    or tidbits, drained, juice
    reserved and divided
1 T. Dijon mustard

Unroll crescent rolls; set aside. Wrap one strip of ham and one strip of cheese around 2 pineapple chunks or 2 to 3 tidbits. Place on the widest part of a crescent roll; roll up. Repeat; arrange on baking sheet. Bake at 375 degrees for 12 to 15 minutes, until golden. Meanwhile, combine mustard and reserved juice in a saucepan. Cook over medium-high heat until thickened, stirring frequently, about 10 minutes. Chop desired amount of remaining pineapple; stir into sauce. Serve sauce with crescents. Makes 8.

Serve a variety of different cheeses at your get-together...perfect for guests to nibble on! Line a white-washed basket with a cheerful napkin and fill it with assorted cheeses and crackers.

Curry Vegetable Dip

Lynnette Jones
East Flat Rock, NC

I have made this simple recipe for quite some time and it is always a favorite. Be sure to allow time for it to chill to blend the flavors together. Serve with your favorite sliced fresh vegetables.

1 c. mayonnaise
1 t. prepared horseradish
1 t. white vinegar

1 t. onion, grated
1/2 t. curry powder

Combine all ingredients in a bowl; mix well. Cover and refrigerate for 4 hours to overnight to allow flavors to blend. Makes 15 servings.

Southwest Hummus

Jill Ball
Highland, UT

My family loves hummus, all kinds. I'll mix up a batch and it's gone before I sit down! Serve with sliced vegetables, tortilla strips or your favorite crackers.

2 15-oz. cans garbanzo beans,
   drained and rinsed
1 c. canned roasted red peppers,
   drained

2 T. taco seasoning mix
2 t. olive oil

Add all ingredients to a food processor. Purée until mixture is mostly smooth but still a little chunky. Cover and chill until serving time. Makes 24 servings.

Nestle a bowl of creamy dip inside a larger bowl filled with crushed ice to keep it cool and tasty.

SPEEDY Snacks & Appetizers

Sharon's Homemade Onion Dip

Sharon Jones
Oklahoma City, OK

This is by far one of the best homemade dips I've tasted.
There is never any left and everyone wants the recipe!

2 T olive oil
1-1/2 c. yellow onions, diced
1/4 t. kosher salt
1-1/2 c. sour cream

3/4 c. mayonnaise
1/4 t. garlic powder
1/4 t. white pepper

Heat oil in a skillet over medium heat. Add onions; sprinkle with salt. Cook until caramelized and golden, stirring occasionally, about 20 minutes. Remove from heat; set aside to cool. Mix remaining ingredients in a serving bowl; stir in cooled onions. Cover and refrigerate; stir before serving. Makes 2 to 2-1/2 cups.

Roasted Red Pepper Spread

Stephanie Dardani-D'Esposito
Ravena, NY

My cousin Virginia always brings these delicious peppers to family gatherings. They are great served on toasted Italian bread, or in an antipasto.

2 24-oz. jars roasted red
   peppers in water, drained
2 T. fresh parsley, chopped
1 clove garlic, minced

2 T. olive oil
1 t. balsamic vinegar
salt to taste

Combine all ingredients except salt in a serving bowl; mix well. Cover and refrigerate for 2 hours before serving; add salt to taste. Makes 8 servings.

Scooped-out sweet peppers make fun containers for dips and sauces.

Easiest-Ever Chicken Wings

Michelle Geraghty
Whitman, MA

So simple and easy! My mom used to make this recipe with skin-on chicken breasts, but I found it easier to use chicken wings and serve as an appetizer. People think I am leaving something out when I tell them the recipe, because it is so simple. They are good cold the next day too...if there are any left! They are one of my most-requested appetizers.

12 to 24 chicken wings,
   tips removed

garlic salt and dried oregano
   to taste

Line the inside of a broiler pan with aluminum foil. Spray broiler pan rack with non-stick vegetable spray. Arrange chicken wings on broiler pan, fitting as many as possible without crowding the wings. Sprinkle with garlic salt and oregano. Place on oven rack in the center of oven. Bake at 400 degrees for 25 to 30 minutes. Turn oven to broil, keeping pan in the center of the oven. Broil for 5 to 10 minutes, until skin is golden, watching carefully to avoid burning. Serves 6 to 8.

"R" Family Punch

Brenda Rogers
Atwood, CA

Oh, the memories of being a kid and drinking this punch at family reunions and get-togethers! My mom never made it at home, but my grandmother and aunts made it whenever we got together. Red punch moustaches on all the cousins!

8 c. cold water
1 env. unsweetened red punch
   drink mix

1 c. sugar
12-oz. can frozen orange juice
   concentrate

In a large pitcher, combine water, drink mix and sugar. Stir until sugar dissolves. Add frozen orange juice; stir until completely mixed in. Serve chilled. Makes 2 quarts.

SPEEDY Snacks & Appetizers

Sweet & Spicy Wings

Lisa Ann Panzino DiNunzio
Vineland, NJ

Sweet and spicy...what could be better?

12 chicken wings, separated
2 to 3 T. extra virgin olive oil
sea salt and pepper to taste

1/2 c. hot pepper sauce
1/4 c. honey

Arrange wings on a baking sheet sprayed with non-stick vegetable spray. Brush with olive oil; season with salt and pepper. Bake at 350 degrees until crisp and golden, about 25 minutes. Combine hot sauce and honey in a small bowl; brush over wings. Bake for another 10 minutes. Turn wings; brush with more of sauce mixture. Bake for another 15 to 20 minutes. If a crisper finish is desired, instead of baking the last 15 to 20 minutes, broil for about 3 to 5 minutes. Serves 6.

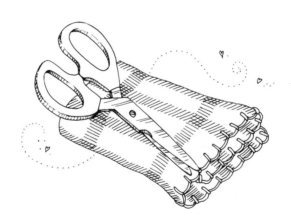

A pair of sturdy kitchen scissors can do a terrific job of sectioning chicken wings. Afterwards, wash the scissors well in soapy water and set on a towel to dry.

Chicken & Ranch Dip

Stacy Luhrs
Southlake, TX

This is the perfect spicy, healthy dip! It's always requested whenever I am going to a house dinner party. It is a must at our huge high school tailgates as well. My friends simply refer to it as "The Dip."

2 12-1/2 oz. cans chicken
    breast, drained
8-oz. container plain Greek
    yogurt

3 T. ranch salad dressing mix
1/2 c. buffalo wing sauce
1/2 c. shredded Cheddar cheese

In a bowl, combine all ingredients except cheese; mix well. Transfer to a lightly greased one-quart casserole dish; top with cheese. Bake, uncovered, at 350 degrees for 20 minutes, until heated through and cheese is melted. Makes 10 servings.

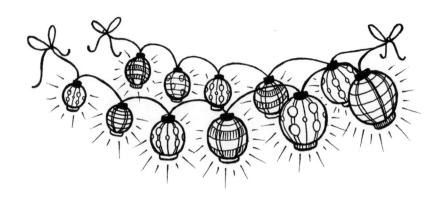

String up twinkly white lights for a backyard
get-together...so festive!

SPEEDY Snacks & Appetizers

Hot Pizza Dip

Rachel Ahrens
Richmond, MI

This delicious recipe is super easy and always a huge hit.
People call ahead and ask me to bring this to parties. Serve
with toasted pita bread or snack crackers.

8-oz. pkg. cream cheese,
  softened
10-3/4 oz. can cream of
  mushroom soup
1 red pepper, diced

8-oz. pkg. shredded mozzarella
  cheese
5-oz. pkg. pepperoni, diced
Garnish: 1/2 c. grated Parmesan
  cheese

In a bowl, blend together all ingredients except garnish. Spoon into an
ungreased 8"x8" baking pan. Sprinkle cheese on top. Bake, uncovered,
at 375 degrees for 30 to 40 minutes, hot and until bubbly throughout.
Serves 10.

Cheesy Reuben Appetizer

Peggy Buckshaw
Stow, OH

This has been enjoyed at many parties and get-togethers
in our home. Serve with cocktail rye bread or rye crackers.

8-oz. pkg. cream cheese,
  softened
1/2 c. Thousand Island salad
  dressing
1/4 lb. deli sliced corned beef,
  chopped

1-1/2 c. shredded Swiss cheese,
  divided
1/2 c. sauerkraut, well drained

In a large bowl, combine cream cheese, dressing, corned beef and one cup
Swiss cheese. Blend well; spread in an ungreased 9" pie plate. Top with
sauerkraut and remaining cheese. Bake, uncovered, at 400 degrees
about 15 minutes, until hot and bubbly around the edges. May make a
day ahead, cover and refrigerate; bake just before serving. Serves 8.

Make your own crunchy pita chips for dipping. Cut pita bread rounds
into triangles, brush lightly with olive oil and sprinkle with garlic
powder. Bake at 350 degrees for a few minutes, until crisp.

Spicy Cheese Shortbread

Zoe Bennett
Columbia, SC

These crisp homemade crackers are delicious all by themselves...even better with your favorite spreads.

8-oz. pkg. shredded sharp
   Cheddar cheese
1-1/2 c. all-purpose flour
3/4 t. dry mustard

1/4 t. cayenne pepper
1/2 c. butter, melted
Optional: 1 T. water

In a large bowl, toss together cheese, flour, mustard and pepper; stir in butter. Knead until dough forms; add water if dough feels dry. Divide into 2 balls. On a floured surface, roll out each ball 1/4-inch thick. Cut out with desired cookie cutters. Place on ungreased baking sheets. Bake at 375 degrees for 10 to 12 minutes, until lightly golden. Cool on a wire rack. Makes about 3 dozen.

Can't-Eat-Just-One Pretzels

Jenessa Yauch
McKeesport, PA

I make these pretzels for every gathering. They are so tasty, everyone asks me for the recipe. So easy...no baking needed!

16-oz. pkg. pretzel nuggets
1/2 c. oil

1-oz. pkg. Italian salad dressing
   mix

Place pretzels in a large bowl. Drizzle with oil; sprinkle with salad dressing mix and toss to coat well. Cover and let stand at room temperature for 8 hours or overnight, tossing occasionally. Makes 15 servings.

Fill a large galvanized tub with ice, then nestle bottled drinks in the ice to keep chilled. Tie a bottle opener to the tub's handle with a ribbon. Everyone can help themselves!

Anna's Italian Twists

Julie Ann Perkins
Anderson, IN

These are great for any occasion and are especially good at the holidays. You might want to make a double batch... they disappear quickly!

1/2 c. pancetta or bacon, finely chopped
13-oz. tube refrigerated pizza dough
1 egg white, lightly beaten

1/4 c. grated Parmesan cheese
2 t. fresh rosemary, chopped, or 1 t. dried rosemary
pepper to taste

In a skillet over medium heat, cook pancetta or bacon until crisp; remove to a paper towel and set aside. Unroll pizza dough and brush with egg white. Sprinkle with pancetta, Parmesan cheese, rosemary and pepper. Fold dough in half horizontally; roll with a rolling pin to lightly seal. Cut into 1/2-inch strips. Lift each strip gently and twist. Place on a parchment paper-lined baking pan. Bake at 425 degrees for 5 to 6 minutes, until crisp and golden. Makes 8 servings.

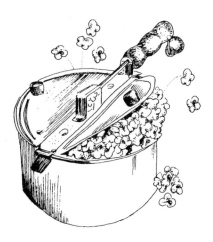

Pizza popcorn...a crunchy snack that's ready in a jiffy! Combine 1/4 cup grated Parmesan cheese, 2 teaspoons each Italian seasoning and paprika, and one teaspoon each onion powder and garlic powder. Sprinkle over 8 cups of buttered popcorn, add salt to taste and toss to mix well.

Amaretto Cheese Spread

Judy Henfey
Cibolo, TX

A simple recipe for the Christmas or New Year's appetizer table.
Serve with thinly sliced apples and pears. Delicious!

8-oz. pkg. cream cheese,
  softened
1/4 c. amaretto liqueur,
  or 1/2 to 1 t. almond extract

2-1/2 oz. pkg. slivered almonds
1-1/2 t. butter

In a bowl, blend together cream cheese and liqueur or extract. Form into a ball; wrap in plastic wrap. Chill until firm. In a small skillet, sauté almonds in butter over medium heat. Shortly before serving time, roll ball in almonds. Serve at room temperature. Makes 4 to 6 servings.

Creamy Fruit Dip

Trina Peterson
Overland Park, KS

This dip is especially good with apples, strawberries, grapes and
bananas. For a lighter option, use 1/3 less fat cream cheese.

1/2 c. cream cheese, softened
6-oz. container vanilla or
  plain yogurt

1/4 c. sugar
1/4 t. vanilla

In a small bowl, combine all ingredients. Blend together with a spatula or whisk until smooth. Cover and chill until ready to serve. Serves 8.

Dip to go! Set out your favorite dips, spooned into portion-size plastic cups. Even layered dips can be served this way. Set the cups in the center of a platter, surrounded by snack chips and vegetable slices.

SPEEDY Snacks & Appetizers

Lemony Ricotta Whip

Jill Ball
Highland, UT

This is a unique dip and a fan favorite...I usually find someone scraping the bowl clean! Serve with sliced bread or crackers.

2 c. whole-milk ricotta cheese
1/4 c. whipping cream
zest of 1 lemon

1 t. olive oil
1/8 t. red pepper flakes

Combine ricotta, cream and lemon zest in a bowl. Beat with an electric mixer on medium speed for 5 minutes, or until light and fluffy. Transfer into a serving bowl; drizzle with oil and stir in red pepper flakes. Makes 12 servings.

Freeze your own crystal-clear party ice cubes. Bring a tea kettle of tap water to a boil. Let it cool to room temperature and pour into ice cube trays. Pop ice cubes into a gallon-size plastic freezer bag until party time.

Crab Salad Spread

Tena Stollar
Kensington, OH

I have used this recipe for years! Everyone loves it. It is so very easy and delicious. Serve with your favorite crackers.

1 lb. imitation crabmeat, finely chopped
1/2 c. sweet onion, finely chopped
2 stalks celery, finely chopped
1 c. sliced almonds, broken
mayonnaise to taste

Combine all ingredients in a large bowl, adding mayonnaise to desired consistency. Mix well. Cover and refrigerate overnight to allow flavors to blend. Makes 8 to 10 servings.

Make a delicious party buffet even more inviting...arrange inverted cake pans or bowls on the table to create different levels. Cover all with a tablecloth and set food platters on top.

SPEEDY **Snacks & Appetizers**

Shrimp Spread

JoAlice Patterson-Welton
Lawrenceville, GA

A great and easy appetizer for when company is coming!
Serve with crackers.

2 6-oz. cans medium shrimp,
    drained
8-oz. pkg. cream cheese,
    softened

1 c. mayonnaise
6 green onions, chopped
3 T. lemon juice

Rinse shrimp under cold water; drain well and chop coarsely. In a
serving bowl, combine shrimp with remaining ingredients; blend well.
Cover and chill for several hours. Serves 8 to 10.

Touchdown Hot Clam Dip

Julie Ann Perkins
Anderson, IN

Serve with pita wedges or your favorite crackers.

8-oz. pkg. cream cheese,
    softened
5-oz. jar sharp pasteurized
    process cheese spread

6-1/2 oz. can minced clams,
    drained
1 bunch green onions, finely
    chopped

Mix all ingredients together in a lightly greased one-quart casserole
dish. Bake, uncovered, at 350 degrees for 20 minutes. Serve warm.
Serves 6 to 8.

Large scallop shells make fun serving containers for seafood dishes.
Use shells you've found on a beach vacation or check party
supply stores for dinner-ready shells.

Texas Queso Dip

Amy Shilliday
San Antonio, TX

The hot pork in this dip really spices things up!

1 lb. hot ground pork sausage,
    browned and drained
32-oz. pkg. pasteurized process
    cheese spread, cubed

10-oz. can diced tomatoes with
    green chiles
1/2 c. milk
white corn tortilla chips

Combine all ingredients except tortilla chips in a slow cooker. Cover and cook on low setting until cheese is melted, about 2 hours. Serve with tortilla chips. Makes 10 to 12 servings.

Easy Nacho Chicken Dip

Laura Flood
Markleville, IN

We like to add sliced jalapeños to this dip! So easy
and quick. Serve with tortilla chips.

12-1/2 oz. can chicken, drained
10-3/4 oz. can Cheddar cheese
    soup
1/2 c. sour cream

1/2 c. plus 2 T. milk
1-1/4 oz. pkg. taco seasoning
    mix
Optional: sliced jalapeño peppers

Mix all ingredients in a bowl. Transfer to a small slow cooker. Cover and cook on low setting for 2 to 3 hours, until hot and bubbly. Makes 6 servings.

May our house always be too small to hold all of our friends.
– Myrtle Reed

Chicken-Bacon Ranch Spread

Brianna Orris
Hebron, IN

This is a spin on the classic chicken salad spread. I love ranch dressing and added it to this one day, and it was so good I had to share it. Spread on crackers or bread slices, or serve as a chip dip.

3 slices bacon, halved
2 5-oz. cans chicken breast,
　drained

3 T. ranch salad dressing mix
1/4 c. sour cream
1/4 c. mayonnaise

Arrange bacon slices on a baking sheet. Bake at 375 degrees for 10 minutes, or until crisp. Drain; crumble into bite-size pieces and set aside. Place chicken in a bowl and shred finely with fork. Add bacon and remaining ingredients; mix well. Cover and chill for 30 minutes before serving. Serves 6.

Bite-size sandwiches are perfect for parties...guests can take as much or as little as they wish. Set out a slow cooker filled with scrumptious pulled pork or shredded chicken alongside a basket of slider buns. Add pickles, chopped onion and other favorite fixings.

Cheesy Mexican Bean Dip

Tammy Navarro
Littleton, CO

I love cheese dip and also love bean dip...this combines both. It's yummy! Use your favorite salsa. Serve with tortilla chips.

10-3/4 oz. can nacho cheese
   soup
11-oz. can sweet corn and diced
   peppers

16-oz. jar favorite salsa
9-oz. can mild or spicy bean dip
3/4 c. regular or non-alcoholic
   beer

Combine all ingredients in a 3-quart slow cooker; do not drain corn. Stir well. Cover and cook on low setting for one to 2 hours, until heated through. Stir again; serve warm. Makes 10 servings.

Are the kids having friends over for snacks? Bright-colored plastic flying disks make great no-spill holders for flimsy paper plates. Afterwards, everyone can take them home as keepsakes.

SPEEDY Snacks & Appetizers

Touchdown Cheese Ball

Sharon Wantland
Menomonee Falls, WI

We are football fans and this is fun to eat during the game.

4 slices bacon, crisply cooked
   and chopped
2 8-oz. pkgs. cream cheese,
   softened
1-oz. pkg. ranch salad
   dressing mix

2-1/2 c. shredded Cheddar
   cheese
1-1/2 c. chopped pecans

In a large bowl, combine all ingredients except nuts. Mix well; form into a ball. Roll in chopped pecans. Wrap in plastic wrap; chill until serving time. Serves 8.

Taco Meatballs

Judy Lange
Imperial, PA

Kids and teenagers love this appetizer. It's fast and easy for reunions, graduations and get-togethers.

2 lbs. ground beef
2 eggs, beaten

1-oz. pkg. taco seasoning mix

Combine all ingredients in a large bowl. Mix well and shape into small meatballs. Placed on an aluminum foil-lined rimmed baking sheet. Bake at 375 degrees for 15 minutes, or until browned; drain. Transfer to a serving platter; insert a toothpick in each meatball. Makes 20 servings.

March 28 is National Something-on-a-Stick Day! Kids will giggle at a meal of meatballs and veggies served on skewers. For dessert, serve up fruit cubes and marshmallows on sticks, with hot fudge sauce for dipping. Such fun!

Caramel Toffee Apple Dip

Marlene Burns
Sebring, FL

So easy! Serve with crisp apple wedges and vanilla wafers.

12-oz. container whipped
   cream cheese
1-1/4 c. caramel apple dip

8-oz. pkg. milk chocolate
   English toffee bits

Spread cream cheese on a serving dish. Layer with caramel dip;
sprinkle with toffee bits. Makes 4-1/4 cups.

Cranberry-Pineapple Dip

Barbara Topp
Holly Springs, NC

Dried cranberries add a festive touch, making this a great recipe
to serve around the holidays. Serve with crackers.

1-1/2 c. shredded Swiss cheese
8-oz. pkg. cream cheese,
   softened
2/3 c. dried cranberries

8-oz. can crushed pineapple,
   partially drained
1/2 c. sliced almonds

Combine all ingredients except almonds in an ungreased 2-quart
casserole dish. Mix well; sprinkle almonds on top. Bake, uncovered, at
350 degrees for 20 to 25 minutes. Serve warm. Makes 8 servings.

Flea markets offer an amazing variety of table serving pieces
for entertaining! Look for vintage china, casseroles and jelly-jar
glasses to add old-fashioned charm to your dinner table.

Puppy Chow

Janet Maynard
Perry, FL

Just for people, of course! If you like chocolate and
peanut butter, you'll love this old favorite.

8 c. bite-size crispy rice
   cereal squares
1/2 c. butter

1 c. semi-sweet chocolate chips
1/2 c. creamy peanut butter
2 c. powdered sugar, divided

Add cereal to a large heat-proof bowl; set aside. In a heavy saucepan over medium heat, melt butter, chocolate chips and peanut butter. Stir until smooth; pour over cereal. Toss to coat well and let cool. Add one cup powdered sugar to a one-gallon plastic zipping bag. Transfer cereal to bag; add remaining powdered sugar and shake bag to coat. Store in an airtight container. Makes 8 to 10 servings.

For fun party favors, fill clear plastic cups with crunchy snack mix.
Seal with sheets of colorful plastic wrap to keep the goodies inside.
Heap the cups in a basket...guests can choose a favorite to take home.

169

Summertime Peach Punch

Sarah Slaven
Strunk, KY

*As a peach lover, this punch is a favorite. My husband
says it's his favorite summertime drink.*

59-oz. container peach punch
   fruit drink
11.3-oz. can apricot nectar

1-1/2 c. sugar, or more to taste
1 ltr. lemon-lime soda
Garnish: vanilla ice cream

In a large punch bowl, combine peach punch and apricot nectar. Add
sugar and stir until dissolved, about 5 minutes. Cover and chill. Just
before serving, add soda and several scoops of ice cream. Makes 12 to
15 servings.

Green Tea Limeade

Jennie Gist
Gooseberry Patch

Refreshing and not too sweet!

2 c. boiling water
4 green tea bags
2 12-oz. cans frozen limeade
   concentrate

Garnish: lime wedges

In a teapot, combine boiling water and tea bags. Let stand for
10 minutes. Discard tea bags; let tea cool slightly. In a large pitcher,
prepare frozen limeade according to package directions. Stir in tea;
cover and chill. Garnish with lime wedges. Serves 20.

Pick up a dozen pint-size
Mason jars for entertaining...
they're fun and practical for
serving frosty beverages.

Strawberry-Lemonade Punch

Cassie Hooker
La Porte, TX

We make this delicious punch for bridal showers, baby showers, and other get-togethers. It calls for frozen, thawed strawberries, but we have used fresh ones also.

6-oz. can frozen lemonade
    concentrate, thawed
6-oz. can frozen limeade
    concentrate, thawed
6-oz. can frozen orange juice
    concentrate, thawed

3 c. cold water
2 10-oz. pkgs. frozen sliced
    strawberries, thawed
2 ltrs. ginger ale, chilled

In a large pitcher, combine frozen juices, cold water and strawberries. Stir well; cover and chill if not serving immediately. At serving time, add ginger ale and stir gently. Serve immediately. Makes one gallon.

For a fruit-studded ice ring that won't dilute your holiday punch, arrange sliced oranges, lemons and limes in a ring mold. Pour in a small amount of punch and freeze until set. Add enough punch to fill mold and freeze until solid. To turn out, dip mold carefully in warm water.

Betty's Bourbon Cocktail Franks
Mary Muchowicz
Elk Grove Village, IL

My Aunt Betty always used to make this appetizer for holiday parties. Everyone loved them! I've been making them for our family get-togethers and they are as popular as ever.

32-oz. bottle catsup
1 c. brown sugar, packed
1/2 c. grape jelly
3/4 c. bourbon
48-oz. pkg. cocktail franks or mini smoked sausages

Combine catsup, brown sugar, jelly and bourbon in a large heavy saucepan. Simmer over very low heat, stirring often, for 1-1/2 hours. Meanwhile, in a separate large saucepan, cover franks or sausages with water. Bring to a boil over medium heat; simmer for 10 to 15 minutes and drain. Add franks or sausages to sauce; heat through. Transfer to a slow cooker set on low, with a slotted spoon and toothpicks for serving. Serves 12.

Good friends are like stars.
You may not always see them,
but you always know they are there.
– Unknown

SPEEDY Snacks & Appetizers

Bacon-Wrapped Cocktail Sausages
Charlotte Smith
Alexandria, PA

This is the best and easiest appetizer I've made in a very long time.
It's so simple and I promise they will disappear very quickly.

1 lb. bacon, cut into 1/4 slices
14-oz. pkg. mini smoked
   sausages

2 c. brown sugar, packed
1/2 c. butter, melted

Wrap a quarter-slice of bacon around each sausage. Arrange sausages
seam-side down in an ungreased 13"x9" baking pan. Sprinkle with
brown sugar; drizzle with butter. Bake, uncovered, at 350 degrees for
20 to 30 minutes, until hot and bacon is done. Serves 18.

Hawaiian Meatballs
Teri Lindquist
Gurnee, IL

These yummy meatballs can keep warm in
a slow cooker until ready to serve.

2 16-oz. pkgs. frozen meatballs
10-oz. jar pineapple preserves

8-oz. bottle barbecue sauce

Place meatballs in a slow cooker. In a bowl, stir together preserves and
sauce; pour over meatballs. Gently stir to combine. Cover and cook on
low setting for 2 to 3 hours, stirring gently once or twice, until
meatballs are hot. Serve with toothpicks. Makes 10 servings.

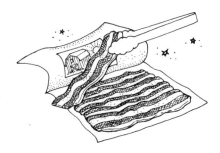

To separate bacon slices easily, first let the package stand
at room temperature for about 20 minutes.

Ann's Fall Pumpkin Dip

Leona Krivda
Belle Vernon, PA

A very nice dip for fall! I have sampled a lot of pumpkin dips, but I got this one from family and it is the best one I ever had. Serve with graham crackers, gingersnaps.

15-oz. can pumpkin
5-oz. pkg. instant vanilla
   pudding mix
1/2 t. pumpkin pie spice

1/4 t. cinnamon
16-oz. container frozen whipped
   topping, thawed

In a large bowl, combine pumpkin, dry pudding mix and spices. Beat well with a mixer on medium speed. Fold in whipped topping to blend well. Transfer to a serving bowl; cover and chill. Garnish with additional cinnamon at serving time. Makes 3 cups.

Peanut Butter Dip

Paula Weaver
Steeleville, IL

This dip is great take to parties or enjoy as a special treat at home. It's a little different and good! Serve with apple slices and graham crackers...I like the teddy bear-shaped crackers!

1 c. creamy peanut butter
8-oz. container vanilla yogurt

1 to 2 t. maple syrup or honey

Mix together all ingredients in a bowl. If too thick, stir in a little more yogurt. May adjust the sweetness with more syrup or honey. Makes 2 cups.

Fill up a big party tray with crisp fresh veggies for dipping... calorie-counting friends will thank you!

EASY-AS-PIE
Desserts

Momma's Pink Cloud Pie

Beckie Apple
Grannis, AR

I have such fond memories of my mother who was a great cook and baker. From a very early age, I remember that Friday was my mom's day for pie making. We lived within walking distance of both sets of grandparents, so Mom would send my brother and me to deliver a fresh-baked pie to them. I still remember the experience of delivering those wonderful smelling pies! Her Pink Cloud Pie was one of my very favorites. I had no idea at the time how quick & easy it was to make.

1 c. boiling water
2 3-oz. pkgs. strawberry or
   cherry gelatin mix
1 c. ice cubes

12-oz. container frozen whipped
   topping, thawed
9-inch graham cracker crust

In a large bowl, combine boiling water and gelatin mix; stir thoroughly until dissolved. Add ice cubes; stir until all ice is dissolved. Cover and refrigerate for 20 minutes. With an electric mixer on medium speed, beat whipped topping into gelatin until smooth. Spoon into crust. Cover and chill for one to 2 hours before serving. Makes 6 to 8 servings.

A pretty saucer that has lost its teacup makes a useful spoon rest to set by the stovetop.

EASY-AS-PIE
Desserts

Best Key Lime Pie

Joyceann Dreibelbis
Wooster, OH

One of the best Key lime pies ever! I am always asked for the recipe.
Tastes just like the pies made in Key West...delicious! It's fine
to use low-fat or fat-free condensed milk, if you like.

2 14-oz. cans sweetened
   condensed milk
1/2 c. sour cream
3/4 c. Key lime juice

1 T. lime zest
9-inch graham cracker crust
Optional: whipped cream,
   lime slices

In a bowl, combine condensed milk, sour cream, lime juice and zest;
mix well. Spoon into crust. Bake at 350 degrees for 8 to 10 minutes,
until tiny pinhole bubbles burst on the surface of the pie. Do not allow
to brown. Chill thoroughly before serving. Garnish with whipped cream
and lime slices, if desired. Serves 6 to 8.

Tropical Cheesecake

Prestie Roach
Huddleston, VA

Super easy...no baking needed! Welcome at any summer party.

1/2 c. powdered sugar
8-oz. pkg. cream cheese,
   softened
8-oz. can crushed pineapple,
   well drained

18-oz. container frozen whipped
   topping, thawed
9-inch graham cracker crust

Sift powdered sugar into a large bowl; add cream cheese. Beat with an
electric mixer on medium speed until fluffy. Add pineapple; stir well.
Fold in whipped topping. Spread into crust. Cover and chill at least
one hour. Makes 6 to 8 servings.

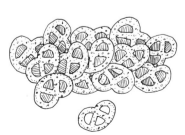

Add a scrumptious salty-sweet contrast
to your favorite pie recipe with a pretzel
crust. Mix 1-1/2 cups finely crushed
pretzel crumbs, 1/4 cup sugar and
1/2 cup melted butter; press into a pie
plate. Chill for 20 minutes before filling.

177

Chocolate Eclair Cake

Danyel Martin
Madisonville, KY

This is the easiest no-bake cake you can make! Great for any occasion. My family loves it!

4-1/2 c. milk
2 5-1/4 oz. pkgs. instant vanilla
pudding mix
8-oz. container frozen whipped
topping, thawed

14.4-oz. pkg. honey graham
crackers
16-oz. can chocolate frosting

In a large bowl, whisk milk and pudding mix for 2 minutes, or until dissolved and smooth. Add whipped topping a little at a time. Blend until completely mixed together and smooth; set aside. Arrange a single layer of graham crackers in an ungreased 13"x9" baking pan. Spoon half of pudding mixture over crackers. Arrange a second single layer of crackers on top of pudding mixture. Spoon remaining pudding mixture over crackers. Arrange a third single layer of crackers on top; set aside. Uncover frosting container; microwave on high for 45 seconds. Frosting will be hot. Pour frosting over crackers; spread until crackers are completely covered. Cover; keep refrigerated. Makes 12 servings.

Seize the moment. Think of all those women on
the Titanic who waved off the dessert cart.
– Erma Bombeck

Mississippi Mud Pie

Vickie
Gooseberry Patch

Irresistibly delicious...an easy make-ahead too.

20 chocolate sandwich cookies, crushed
1/3 c. butter, melted
1 qt. chocolate, coffee or vanilla ice cream, softened
8-oz. container frozen whipped topping, thawed and divided
3/4 c. thick fudge sauce, chilled
Optional: additional crushed cookies, slivered almonds

Combine cookie crumbs and melted butter in a bowl; press into a 9" pie plate. Bake at 350 degrees for 10 minutes; cool completely. Transfer ice cream to a large bowl; stir until smooth. Fold in 1-3/4 cups whipped topping; refrigerate remaining topping. Cover and freeze until firm, stirring occasionally. Spoon ice cream mixture into cooled crust. Cover and freeze for several hours, until completely firm. Spread cold fudge sauce over pie; freeze for one hour. To serve, let stand at room temperature for 10 minutes. Garnish with remaining topping, remaining crushed cookies and almonds, if desired. Serves 8.

Joshua's Butterscotch Cake

Linda Smith
Fountain Hills,, AZ

This is my son's favorite cake and it is so easy to make. Serve as either a morning coffee cake or a dinner dessert. Needs no icing and is very moist. What more could you want?

18-1/2 oz. pkg. yellow cake mix
4 3-1/4 oz. cups butterscotch pudding
2 eggs, beaten
6-oz. pkg. butterscotch chips
1/3 c. sugar

In a large bowl, combine cake mix, pudding and eggs; beat until well mixed. Pour batter into a greased 13"x9" baking pan. Sprinkle butterscotch chips and sugar over batter and press in. Bake at 350 degrees for 30 to 35 minutes; do not overbake. Makes 12 servings.

Aunt Betty's Pecan Squares

Kay Kingsley
Indianapolis, IN

My family always looked forward to our visits to see Aunt Betty and her family over the holidays. We were always happy to find Pecan Squares in her cookie jar. We have made them countless times... hard to stop eating them!

1 c. butter, softened	2 c. all-purpose flour
1 c. brown sugar, packed	1 c. chopped pecans
1 egg, separated	1/2 t. salt

In a large bowl, blend butter and brown sugar. Add egg yolk; beat until fluffy. Add remaining ingredients except egg white; mix well. With your hands, press dough onto a greased 15"x10" jelly-roll pan, all the way to the edges. Brush with lightly beaten egg white. Bake at 350 degrees for 20 to 25 minutes. Cool slightly; cut into squares. Makes 2 dozen.

Speedy Peanut Butter Cookies

Tiffany Leiter,
Midland, MI

That's correct...there's no flour in these cookies!

1 c. sugar	1 egg
1 c. creamy peanut butter	

Blend all ingredients together; set aside for 5 minutes. Scoop dough with a small ice cream scoop; place 2 inches apart on ungreased baking sheets. Make a crisscross pattern on top of each cookie using the tines of a fork; bake at 350 degrees for 10 to 12 minutes. Cool on baking sheets for 5 minutes; remove to wire rack to finish cooling. Serves 15.

For best results when baking cookies, allow butter and eggs to come to room temperature before using.

EASY-AS-PIE
Desserts

Saltine Cracker Cookies

Jamie Guimaraes
Pittsburgh, PA

I got this recipe years ago from my mom's friend. I started making it as a treat for our youth group at summer camp. Everyone loved it so much, they were all eaten up the first night of camp! Now I make this recipe every year as Christmas gifts for our family and neighbors. I'm always asked for the recipe.

16-oz. pkg. saltine crackers
1 c. butter, melted
1 c. brown sugar, packed

12-oz. pkg. milk chocolate chips
8-oz. pkg. toffee baking bits

Line a large baking sheet with aluminum foil; spray with non-stick vegetable spray. Line baking sheet with saltine crackers; set aside. In a saucepan over medium heat, melt butter with brown sugar; bring to a boil for one minute. Pour mixture over crackers; spread to completely cover all the crackers. Bake at 400 degrees for 7 minutes. Remove from oven; immediately sprinkle chocolate chips evenly over top. When chocolate begins to melt, spread it evenly over all the crackers. Sprinkle toffee bits over chocolate. Cool completely; break into pieces. Makes 2 dozen.

Butter Brickle Cookies

Sandra Monroe
Preston, MD

This cookies are so good and so easy to make using a cake mix.

18-oz. pkg. butter pecan
   cake mix
2 eggs, beaten

1/2 c. margarine, softened
8-oz. pkg. toffee baking bits

In a large bowl, combine dry cake mix and remaining ingredients. Mix well; drop by tablespoonfuls onto greased baking sheets. Bake at 350 degrees for 9 to 10 minutes. Makes 2 to 3 dozen.

Keep crisp cookies crisp and soft cookies chewy in a cookie jar...
separate the layers with sheets of wax paper.

Strawberry Angel Food Cake

Debi McClain
Bennington, IN

My mother loved to make this dessert for church dinners. It's simple to make, since you start with a store-bought angel food cake. It is very refreshing and not as many calories as a regular cake. She wasn't a baker so she was happy to try this recipe. I always think of her when I make this.

12-oz. container frozen whipped
    topping, thawed
14-oz. pkg. strawberry gel

1 angel food cake
1 pt. fresh strawberries, hulled
    and sliced

Combine whipped topping and strawberry gel in a large bowl. Use an electric mixer on low speed to mix well. Spread mixture over cake; arrange strawberries over cake. Refrigerate until serving time. Serves 10 to 12.

Lemon Custard Cake

R. E. Rohlof
Hicksville, OH

Simple to make, yet simply luscious to eat.

1 angel food cake, torn into
    bite-size pieces
1-3/4 oz. pkg. instant lemon
    pudding mix

1-1/2 c. cold milk
1 c. sour cream
21-oz. can cherry pie filling

Arrange cake pieces in an ungreased 13"x9" baking pan; set aside. In a bowl, combine pudding mix, milk and sour cream. Beat with an electric mixer on medium speed until thickened, about 2 to 3 minutes. Spread mixture over cake pieces; top with pie filling. Cover and chill until serving time. Makes 8 to 10 servings.

A real kitchen time-saver! A silicon hot pad can function as trivet, potholder, anti-slip pad for mixing bowls and jar opener.

Desserts

Butter Pecan Peach Cake

Carole Akers
Bellevue, OH

So refreshing in the summer, or serve warm on chilly days...
a yummy treat either way!

29-oz. can sliced peaches
18-1/4 oz. pkg. butter pecan or
    yellow
      cake mix

1/2 c. butter, melted
1 c. chopped pecans
1 c. sweetened flaked coconut

Pour peaches and syrup in the bottom of an ungreased 13"x9" baking pan. Cover with dry cake mix; drizzle butter over the top. Sprinkle with pecans and coconut. Bake, uncovered, at 350 degrees for 30 to 35 minutes. Serves 18 to 24.

Vintage tin cake carriers are so pretty...their colors and patterns add a spot of cheer to kitchens and get-togethers! Keep an eye out for them at flea markets, tag sales and rummage sales.

Oatmeal Crumb Dessert

Becky Kuchenbecker
Ravenna, OH

My mother-in-law gave me this recipe years ago. It's an old standby recipe that's easy to make...delicious, too! I like to change it up with different kinds of pie filling.

2 c. all-purpose flour
2 c. quick-cooking oats, uncooked
1 c. sugar

1/2 t. salt
1 c. butter, softened
21-oz. can cherry pie filling

In a large bowl, mix together flour, oats, sugar, salt and butter into a crumb mixture. Press half of crumb mixture into a lightly greased 13"x9" baking pan. Top with pie filling. Spread remaining crumb mixture on top. Bake at 350 degrees for 45 minutes, or until lightly golden. Makes 12 servings.

At dessert time, set out whipped cream and shakers of cinnamon and cocoa for coffee drinkers. Tea drinkers will love a basket of special teas with honey and lemon slices.

EASY-AS-PIE
Desserts

Frozen Cherry Dessert

Leona Krivda
Belle Vernon, PA

A quick and handy dessert to have on hand. Everyone will like it!

21-oz. can cherry pie filling
8-oz. container frozen whipped
   topping, thawed
14-oz. can sweetened condensed
   milk

8-oz. can crushed pineapple,
   drained
1/2 c. chopped nuts

Mix all ingredients together in a bowl; transfer to a plastic freezer container. Cover and freeze. Let stand at room temperature 15 minutes before serving. Scoop into dessert dishes. Serves 6.

Easy Berry Crumble

Alice Hardin
Antioch, CA

If you want a really, really easy dessert that is yummy and low in calories...this is the one for you. It is delicious!

2 12-oz. pkgs. frozen mixed
   berries

18-1/2 oz. pkg. white cake mix
12-oz. can diet lemon-lime soda

Place frozen berries in a lightly greased 13"x9" baking pan. Sprinkle dry cake mix over berries. Pour soda slowly over cake mix; do not stir. Bake at 350 degrees for about 45 to 50 minutes, until just turning golden. Makes 12 servings.

Take Mom or Grandma along to a farmstand and ask her to share her tried & true fruit recipes with you. You may find a new favorite!

Delicious Banana Toffee Pie

Sandy Ann Ward
Anderson, IN

This is for kids of all ages. Leave the house if you must,
but don't slice into it before chilling!

14-oz. can sweetened condensed
  milk
10-inch deep-dish pie crust,
  baked

2 to 3 ripe bananas,
  diagonally sliced
1 c. whipping cream
Garnish: crushed toffee bits

Pour condensed milk into the top of a double boiler. Cook over
simmering water for about 30 minutes, or until thick and caramel
colored, stirring frequently. Let cool. Pour caramelized milk into baked
pie crust; arrange banana slices on top and set aside. In a deep bowl,
beat cream with an electric mixer on high setting until stiff peaks form.
Spread over banana layer. Garnish with toffee bits. Cover and chill at
least one hour before serving. Serves 6 to 8.

Angel Food Pineapple Cake

Sandra Sullivan
Aurora, CO

A great last-minute dessert! In no time at all, I can whip this up
and serve it with a bowl of fresh berries and some creamy topping.

16-oz. pkg. angel food cake mix
20-oz. can crushed pineapple

Garnish: assorted fresh berries,
  whipped cream

Pour dry cake mix into a large bowl; add pineapple with juice. Mix
well; batter will begin to foam. Spread batter in a 13"x9" baking pan
lightly sprayed with non-stick vegetable spray. Bake at 350 degrees
for 30 minutes. Cut into squares; top with berries and
a dollop of whipped cream. Makes 12 servings.

To toast coconut, place in a dry skillet
over medium-low heat. Cook and stir
until lightly toasted, about 3 minutes.

Piña Colada Cake

Joyceann Dreibelbis
Wooster, OH

Only four ingredients are needed to make this fabulous tropical dessert. Very light and refreshing!

16-oz. pkg. angel food cake mix
16-oz. can unsweetened crushed
   pineapple

8-oz. container frozen fat-free
   whipped topping, thawed
1/2 c. toasted flaked coconut

In a large bowl, stir together dry cake mix and pineapple with juice. Pour batter into a 13"x9" baking pan sprayed with non-stick vegetable spray. Bake at 350 degrees for 20 to 25 minutes, until a toothpick inserted in center tests almost clean. Cool cake completely on a wire rack. Spread whipped topping over cake. Sprinkle with coconut. Cover and refrigerate until serving time. Makes 16 servings.

A neighborhood dessert party is a tasty way to get together with nearby friends! Invite everyone to tie on an apron and bring their best-loved cake or pie.

Malted Milk Ball Lover's Delight

Pat Beach
Fisherville, KY

This dessert reminds me of the chocolate malts served years ago at the soda fountain shops that I frequented as a child.

2 c. graham cracker crumbs
1/2 c. margarine, melted
1/2 gal. vanilla ice cream, melted
12-oz. pkg. malted milk balls,
   crushed

16-oz. container frozen whipped
   topping, thawed

In a bowl, mix graham cracker crumbs and melted margarine together. Press into an ungreased 13"x9" baking pan; cover and freeze until frozen. Pour ice cream over frozen crust. Return to freezer until frozen. In a separate bowl, fold crushed malted milk balls into whipped topping; spread over frozen ice cream. Cover and return to freezer until frozen. Cut into squares and serve. Makes 12 to 15 servings.

No time to bake today? Turn store-bought cookies into extra-special treats. Melt chocolate chips, then dip in half of each cookie...pretty with white chocolate too. Decorate with sprinkles or chopped nuts as you like.

EASY-AS-PIE
Desserts

Grandma's Butter Cake

Donna Ricci
Logansport, IN

Mother made this cake and we ate it hot!

16-oz. pkg. pound cake mix
4 eggs, divided
1/2 c. butter, melted and slightly
  cooled

8-oz. pkg. cream cheese,
  softened
16-oz. pkg. powdered sugar

In a large bowl, combine dry cake mix, 2 eggs and melted butter. Mix well; press into a lightly greased 13"x9" baking pan. In a separate bowl, blend together cream cheese, remaining eggs and powdered sugar. Spread over batter. Bake at 350 degrees for 30 to 35 minutes, until golden. Makes 12 servings.

Chocolate Pudding Cake

Annette Ceravolo
Hoover, AL

*A double dose of chocolate that's been a
family favorite for years!*

18-1/2 oz. pkg. devil's food
  cake mix
1-1/4 c. water
2 c. milk
2 3.9-oz. pkgs. instant chocolate
  pudding mix

1/3 c. sugar
Optional: whipped topping or
  vanilla ice cream

Prepare cake according to package directions. Pour batter into a greased 13x9" baking pan; set aside. In a separate bowl, combine water, milk, pudding mixes and sugar. Whisk together for 2 minutes, or well blended; pour over batter. Set pan in a larger shallow pan to catch drips. Bake at 350 degrees for 55 minutes to one hour, until a toothpick tests clean. Cool for 20 minutes. "Sauce" on top will thicken slightly as it cools. Serve warm, spooned into bowls and garnished as desired. Makes 12 servings.

Gooey Butter Cookies

Andrea Heyart
Savannah, TX

These cookies have been a Christmas tradition in my family for at least 20 years now. Whoever is in charge of baking always knows to double or triple the recipe. No matter how many are on hand, they will all be devoured well before New Year's Eve!

15-1/4 oz. pkg. golden butter
   cake mix
8-oz. pkg. cream cheese,
   softened

1 egg, beaten
1/2 c. butter, softened
1 t. vanilla extract
Garnish: powdered sugar

In a large bowl, combine all ingredients except powdered sugar. Beat with an electric mixer on high speed until well mixed. Cover and chill for at least 30 minutes. Scoop chilled dough into one-inch balls; roll in powdered sugar. Place on parchment paper-lined baking sheets. Bake at 350 degrees for 9 to 12 minutes, until golden; a little underdone is better than overdone. Let cool. Sprinkle with additional powdered sugar, if desired. Makes 2 dozen.

Double Chocolate Cookies

Meredith Drummond
McAlester, OK

I'm a chocolate lover and this recipe is so good and easy to make.

18-1/4 oz. pkg. chocolate
   cake mix
2 eggs, beaten

2/3 c. oil
2 c. semi-sweet chocolate chips

In a bowl, combine dry cake mix, eggs and oil. Beat well; stir in chips. Roll dough into balls by teaspoonfuls. Place on greased baking sheets. Bake at 350 degrees for 10 minutes. Cool on baking sheets for 2 minutes; remove to a wire rack. Makes 3 dozen.

When baking 2 sheets of cookies at once, swap the top and bottom sheets halfway through the baking time so they will bake more evenly.

EASY-AS-PIE
Desserts

Cake Mix Cookies

Karen Hughes
Newberry, SC

This recipe is so simple and fun so everyone in the family can get involved. We have a lot of fun creating new batches. Just go by the basic recipe and then make cookies for any & all occasions. We have been labeled the best cookie makers in our area. Enjoy!

18-oz. pkg. favorite-flavor
    cake mix
2 eggs, beaten
2 T. water

1/2 c. oil
1 c. chopped candy, nuts or
    dried fruit

In a large bowl, beat together dry cake mix, eggs, water and oil. Fold in choice of candy, nuts or fruit. Drop dough by teaspoonfuls onto ungreased baking sheets. Bake at 350 degrees for 9 to 11 minutes. Makes 3 dozen.

Flavor variations:

- White cake mix with chopped coconut-almond candy bars
- Yellow cake mix with candy-coated chocolates
- Chocolate cake mix with butterscotch chips or candy corn
- Carrot cake mix with raisins and chopped pecans
- Butter pecan cake mix with chopped pecan cookies
- Red velvet cake mix with white chocolate chips

A fast and fun party punch to serve with cookies. Simply combine a 2-liter bottle of chilled soda with a pint of sherbet. Match up flavors... strawberry sherbet with strawberry soda, rainbow sherbet with lemon-lime soda. Yummy!

Fuss-Free Strawberry Bars

Jackie Smulski
Lyons, IL

A quick & easy recipe when you're craving a strawberry-flavored treat. They can also be made with blackberry, peach or raspberry preserves...choose your favorite!

1/2 c. butter, softened
1/2 c. brown sugar, packed
1 egg, beaten

18-1/4 oz. pkg. yellow cake mix
1 c. corn flake cereal, crushed
1 c. strawberry jam or preserves

In a bowl, blend butter and brown sugar until smooth. Add egg and mix well. Gradually stir in dry cake mix and crushed cereal. Set aside 1-1/2 cups of dough for topping. Press remaining dough into a greased 13"x9" baking pan. Carefully spread jam or preserves over dough. Sprinkle with reserved dough; gently press down. Bake at 350 degrees for 30 minutes, or until golden. Cool completely in pan on a wire rack. Cut into bars. Makes 2 dozen.

Shortbread Fingers

Alice Joy Randall
Nacogdoches, TX

I've made this recipe for over 40 years. It is delicious and very easy.

1-1/2 c. all-purpose flour
1/3 c. sugar
1/2 c. butter, softened

1/2 t. vanilla extract
Garnish: powdered sugar

Combine flour, sugar, butter and vanilla in a bowl. Work with your fingers until well blended and a soft dough forms. Press dough evenly into an ungreased 8"x8" baking pan. Pierce well all over with a fork. Bake at 350 degrees for 25 minutes, or until lightly golden. Cut into 32 bars; sprinkle with powdered sugar. Cool completely in pan on a wire rack. Makes 32 cookies.

Grape Jelly Granola Bars

Janis Parr
Ontario, Canada

These no-bake bars are a yummy favorite of kids and adults alike. They are very tasty and moist.

1/2 c. butterscotch chips
2/3 c. grape jelly
2 c. granola cereal

1 c. quick-cooking oats, uncooked
1/2 c. chopped peanuts

Melt butterscotch chips in a saucepan over low heat, stirring constantly. Add grape jelly and stir until blended. Remove from heat. Add granola, dry oats and peanuts; stir until well coated. Spread evenly in a greased 9"x9" baking pan. Cover and refrigerate until firm. Cut into bars. Makes 9 bars.

Macaroon Kisses

Judy Lange
Imperial, PA

An old-time easy & delicious cookie for graduations, showers and parties. Looks beautiful on a cookie platter!

14-oz. can sweetened condensed milk
2 t. vanilla extract
1 t. almond extract

2 7-oz. pkgs sweetened flaked coconut
48 milk chocolate drops or stars

In a large bowl combine condensed milk and extracts. Stir in coconut. Drop by teaspoonfuls onto parchment paper-lined baking sheets. Slightly flatten with a spoon. Bake at 325 degrees for 15 to 17 minutes, until golden. Remove from oven; press a chocolate into centers of macaroons. Remove from baking sheets onto a wire rack; cool completely. Store loosely covered at room temperature. Makes 4 dozen.

Slice bar cookies into one-inch squares and set them in frilly paper candy cups. Guests will love sampling "just a bite" of several different treats.

Mom's Strawberry Pie

Joyce Borrill
Utica, NY

My family referred to this pie as the "Pride of Summer." When my nephew was born, Mom made this pie and we all raved about it so, she told us, "You bring the berries and I'll make the pies." We did... and she made 9 pies in all! Not a crumb left.

1 qt. fresh strawberries, hulled
   and divided
3 T. cornstarch

1 c. sugar
9-inch pie crust, baked
Garnish: whipped cream

Set aside 4 to 6 strawberries; mash remaining berries in a saucepan over medium heat. Add cornstarch and sugar; bring to a boil for one minute. Halve reserved berries and add to pan. Simmer for 10 minutes, until thickened. Spoon into baked pie crust; cover and refrigerate. At serving time, garnish with a dollop of whipped cream. Makes 5 to 6 servings.

January 5 is National Whipped Cream Day. Just about any dessert is made better with a dollop of whipped cream, so choose your favorite and celebrate with the family!

EASY-AS-PIE
Desserts

Raspberry & Peach Pound Cake

Ramona Storm
Gardner, IL

Makes a very pretty and tasty dessert. Dollop on some whipped cream and add some fresh raspberries, if you like.

10-oz. pkg. frozen raspberries, thawed
1 T. cornstarch
1 T. sugar

15-oz. can sliced cling peaches, well drained
6 slices pound cake, packaged or homemade

In a saucepan over medium heat, combine raspberries, cornstarch and sugar. Bring to a boil, stirring constantly. Set aside to cool. In a bowl, mash peaches slightly. To serve, place slices of pound cake on dessert plates. Top with peaches and drizzle warm raspberry sauce over top. Makes 6 servings.

Quickie Pineapple-Cherry Dessert

Heather Sinclair
Ontario, Canada

An oh-so-easy dessert you're going to love...just dump and bake! Garnish with whipped topping, if you like.

20-oz. can crushed pineapple
18-1/2 oz. pkg. white cake mix

21-oz. can cherry pie filling
1 T. butter, diced

Spread pineapple with juice in a lightly greased 13"x9" baking pan. Top with pie filling; pour dry cake mix evenly over fruit and dot with butter. Bake at 350 degrees for about one hour, until top is crusty and golden. Makes 12 to 16 servings.

Save time when serving ice cream-topped desserts to a party crowd! Scoop ice cream ahead of time and freeze in paper muffin liners.

Peanut Butter Cup Pie

JoAnn Cain
Verden, IL

*My husband loves peanut butter, and when my son was
a child, he always loved peanut butter cups. Both of them
are pleased when I serve this pie!*

3.9-oz. pkg. instant chocolate
   pudding mix
2 c. milk, divided
9-inch pie crust, baked

3.4-oz. pkg. instant vanilla
   pudding mix
1/2 c. creamy peanut butter
Garnish: whipped cream

In a bowl, combine chocolate pudding mix and one cup milk. Whisk
until well mixed; spread in baked pie crust. Repeat with vanilla
pudding mix and remaining milk; stir in peanut butter. Spread over
chocolate layer. Cover and chill for at least one hour. Top servings with
a dollop of whipped cream. Serves 6.

Grandma's Candy Bar Pie

Carolyn Deckard
Bedford, IN

*This is one of so many favorite things Grandma always made for us
at Christmas. For an added delight, she would garnish it with
whipped cream or ice cream. Enjoy...so good!*

6 1.45-oz. chocolate candy bars
   with almonds
17 marshmallows, quartered

1/2 c. milk
1 c. whipping cream
9-inch graham cracker crust

In the top of a double boiler, combine chocolate, marshmallows and
milk. Cook over simmering water until melted; stir until smooth.
Remove from heat. Beat whipping cream in a large bowl until stiff
peaks form. Stir whipped cream into chocolate mixture; pour into crust.
Cover and refrigerate at least 3 hours. May be prepared 2 to 3 days
ahead. Makes 6 to 8 servings.

Chopped or crushed candy bars make a fast & easy topping for frosted
cakes. Try using toffee, caramel or nougat bars...scrumptious!

EASY-AS-PIE Desserts

Easy Chocolate Mint Pie

Kathy Courington
Canton, GA

I was always afraid to make pies until I figured out that with instant pudding mix it's a snap. Easy to make for potlucks and low in calories too. Sometimes I sprinkle the pie with a few mini chocolate chips for fun. A true family favorite!

2 3.9-oz. pkgs. sugar-free
   instant chocolate
   pudding mix
1-1/3 c. instant non-fat dry
   milk powder

2-1/2 c. water
1/2 t. peppermint extract
1 c. frozen light whipped
   topping, thawed and divided
9-inch shortbread cookie crust

In a large bowl, combine dry pudding mixes and dry milk powder. Add water and extract; whisk together well. Blend in 1/2 cup whipped topping. Spread mixture in pie crust. Cover and refrigerate for 30 minutes. Top with remaining topping. Serves 8.

Terrific Toffee Dessert

Pat Beach
Fisherville, KY

I'm so glad my neighbor shared this recipe with me years ago. It's a toffee lover's dream come true!

1-1/2 c. chocolate wafer crumbs
1/4 c. margarine, melted
1/2 gal. vanilla ice cream,
   softened

12 1.4-oz. chocolate-covered
   toffee candy bars, crushed
11-3/4 oz. jar hot fudge sauce,
   warmed

Mix chocolate wafer crumbs and melted margarine in a bowl; press firmly into bottom of an ungreased 13"x9" baking pan. Refrigerate until hardened. Fold crushed toffee bars into softened ice cream. Spread evenly over crust; cover and freeze overnight. At serving time, top with hot fudge sauce; cut into squares. Serves 12 to 15.

Grandma Carter's 5-Cup Salad

Cindy Neel
Gooseberry Patch

This sweet recipe was one of my Great-Grandmother Pearl's.

8-1/4 oz. can mandarin oranges,
   drained
8-oz. can crushed pineapple,
   drained

8-oz. container sour cream
1 c. sweetened flaked coconut
1 c. mini marshmallows

Combine all ingredients in a large serving bowl. Mix well; cover and refrigerate until serving time. Makes 4 to 6 servings.

Orange Ice Cream Dessert

Nancy Lanning
Lancaster, SC

When we were young, my grandmother made this for us and we loved it! It was just like having an orange & cream frozen pop from the ice cream truck that went through our town in the evenings.

3-oz. pkg. orange gelatin mix
1 c. boiling water

2 c. vanilla ice cream, softened

In a bowl, dissolve gelatin mix in boiling water. Gradually add softened ice cream; stir with a whisk until smooth. Spoon into 4 dessert bowls. Cover and chill until set. Serves 4.

To keep a chilled dessert cool on a warm day, just fill a picnic basket with plastic zipping bags full of ice, lay a colorful tea towel over the ice and set the sweets on top.

Daffodil Lemon Dessert

JoAlice Patterson-Welton
Lawrenceville, GA

This is a family recipe that has been around for ages. It's wonderful and light, especially when the summer months arrive. My late mom, Alice, made this dessert whenever she needed something easy yet light and very tasty.

14-oz. can sweetened
   condensed milk
juice of 4 lemons
1/2 c. sugar

16-oz. container whipping
   cream
1 small angel food cake, torn
   into bite-size pieces

In a large bowl, stir together condensed milk, lemon juice and sugar; set aside. In a separate bowl, beat whipping cream with an electric mixer on high speed until stiff peaks form. Fold whipped cream into condensed milk mixture; set aside. Line the bottom of an ungreased 13"x9" baking pan with cake pieces. Pour condensed milk mixture over cake; mix together a little to blend cake into the mixture. Cover and chill for 24 hours before serving. Makes 8 to 10 servings.

Don't hide a pretty glass cake stand in the cupboard! When it's
not in use, show off several of Mom's best dessert plates
or arrange colorful seasonal fruit on top.

Spiced Apple Crumble

Kaela Oates
Waverly, WV

My husband loves anything with apples. This recipe makes it easy for me to surprise him any night of the week!

4 c. apple pie filling
16-1/2 oz. pkg. spice cake mix
1/4 c. butter, melted

Optional: vanilla ice cream
 or whipped cream

Pour pie filling into a buttered 9" round cake pan. Sprinkle dry cake mix evenly over filling. Drizzle melted butter over top; do not stir. Bake at 375 degrees for 35 to 40 minutes. Serve garnished as desired. Makes 6 to 8 servings.

Quick Apple Pie

Patricia Province
Strawberry Plains, TN

This is tasty and truly as easy as apple pie!

2 12-oz. tubes refrigerated
 cinnamon rolls

21-oz. can apple pie filling
Garnish: ice cream

Open one can of cinnamon rolls; set aside icing packet. Unroll each cinnamon roll; place side-by-side in the bottom of a greased 9"x9" baking pan, cinnamon-side up. Rolls should be touching. Spoon pie filling over rolls. Unroll remaining rolls and place each one on top, cinnamon-side down. Bake, uncovered, at 350 degrees for 20 to 25 minutes. Drizzle reserved icing over pie; serve warm with ice cream. Makes 6 servings.

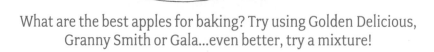

What are the best apples for baking? Try using Golden Delicious, Granny Smith or Gala...even better, try a mixture!

EASY-AS-PIE Desserts

Caramel-Cinnamon Dessert

Wendy Ball
Battle Creek, MI

This lovely treat speaks holidays. Feed a crowd too!

5-oz. pkg. French vanilla instant
    pudding mix
3 c. milk
8-oz. container frozen whipped
    topping, thawed

14-oz. pkg. cinnamon graham
    crackers
16-oz. can caramel frosting

Combine pudding mix and milk in a large bowl; mix well until dissolved. Fold in whipped topping. Line the bottom of an ungreased 13"x9" glass baking pan with whole graham crackers. Spoon half of pudding mixture over crackers. Top pudding mixture with a second layer of crackers; spread remaining pudding over top. Top with remaining crackers; 2 to 3 crackers may be left over. Soften frosting, if necessary; spread over graham crackers. Cover and refrigerate until serving time. Makes 15 to 18 servings.

Create charming cupcake stands from tag-sale teacups and saucers.
Invert each teacup and glue its saucer on top with epoxy glue. So clever!

201

Aunt Patsy's Peach Pie

Kassie Frazier
West Point, TN

My aunt's recipe for peach pie is melt-in-your-mouth good. This recipe has been served at every family gathering for as long as I can remember. And in our large family, you'd better get to this dessert, as we say, while the gettin' is good...otherwise it will be gone!

1/2 c. margarine, melted
2 15-oz. cans sliced peaches
1 c. milk

1-1/2 c. sugar
1-1/2 c. all-purpose flour

Spray a 13"x9" baking pan with non-stick spray; pour melted butter into pan. Cut peach slices into thirds; add peaches with juice to pan and set aside. In a bowl, combine flour, sugar and milk; mix well. Pour batter over peaches; do not stir. Bake at 350 degrees for 50 to 60 minutes, until golden. Makes 6 servings.

No-Guilt Fruit Fluff

Lori Gartzke
Fargo, ND

This dessert or salad tastes so rich, but has virtually no sugar or fat and very few carbs! Try other combinations of fruit and gelatin too. I like to save some pieces of fruit to decorate the top after it has set.

3-oz. pkg. sugar-free orange
  gelatin mix
1 c. boiling water
1/2 c. cold water
3-oz. pkg. sugar-free instant
  vanilla pudding mix

2 10-oz. cans mandarin
  oranges, drained
8-oz. container frozen fat-free
  whipped topping, thawed

In a large bowl, dissolve gelatin mix in boiling water. Add cold water; cover and refrigerate for 15 minutes. Whisk in dry vanilla pudding mix; fold in whipped topping and oranges. Cover and chill. Makes 6 servings.

A tea strainer makes short work of
sifting powdered sugar over desserts.

EASY-AS-PIE
Desserts

Quick & Easy Rhubarb Pie

Abi Buening
Grand Forks, ND

This pie has been in our family for many years. We love it because it is so easy to make...and you couldn't ask for a much tastier pie!

4 to 5 c. rhubarb, chopped
8-inch pie crust, unbaked
1 c. sugar

1/3 c. all-purpose flour
2 c. frozen whipped topping, thawed

Spread rhubarb evenly in unbaked crust; set aside. In a bowl, stir together sugar, flour and whipped topping; spread evenly over rhubarb. Bake at 450 degrees for 10 minutes. Reduce oven to 350 degrees; bake another 30 to 40 minutes longer. Makes 8 servings.

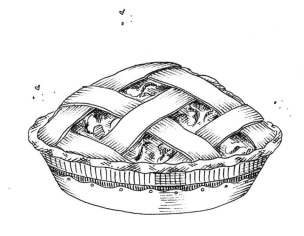

Try sugar-substitute blends made especially for baking to turn out sweet, golden, moist goodies with half the sugar. There's even a brown sugar variety! Be sure to check the package for how to measure correctly.

Fresh Peaches & Strawberry Yogurt Sauce

Wendy Ball
Battle Creek, MI

Can't decide if this makes a good dessert or a good breakfast! It's perfect for either. Our grandkids love both fruits, so it's a win-win. Decorate with fresh strawberries for a delicious and light dessert.

1 c. fresh strawberries, hulled
  and sliced, or raspberries
1/2 c. non-fat vanilla Greek
  yogurt
1 T. sweetener or honey

4 ripe peaches, peeled, pitted
  and sliced
Optional: frozen whipped
  topping

Combine berries, yogurt and sweetener or honey in a blender or food processor. Process until smooth; chill in refrigerator until needed. At serving time, divide peaches among 4 dessert dishes; spoon berry sauce on top. Garnish with a dollop of whipped topping, if desired. Makes 4 servings.

Fresh-picked berries are a special country pleasure. Store them in a colander in the refrigerator to let cold air circulate around them. There's no need to wash them until you're ready to use them.

EASY-AS-PIE
Desserts

Caramelized Bananas

*Judy Lange
Imperial, PA*

*When you are in the mood for something sweet, this will do it!
An easy and yummy dessert to whip up in a jiffy.*

2 T. butter
2 T. brown sugar, packed
1 large ripe banana, sliced
    1/4-inch thick on the
    diagonal

Garnish: vanilla ice cream

Melt butter in a small skillet over medium heat; stir in sugar. Add banana and cook, turning slices, until golden and sauce has formed. Serve over scoops of ice cream. Makes 2 servings.

Warm Cinnamon Apples

*Stefanie St. Pierre
Chatham, MA*

*The ultimate comfort food! Fall is my favorite time of year
and this is always requested as soon as it starts to get
chilly outside. Serve over vanilla ice cream...yum!*

4 McIntosh apples, peeled,
    cored and sliced
1/2 c. light brown sugar, packed
1 t. cinnamon

1/4 t. nutmeg
2 T. water
1 T. butter

In a large bowl, toss together apple slices, brown sugar and spices until all the slices are coated. Combine water and butter in a saucepan over medium heat. Add apple mixture and cook for 8 to 10 minutes, or to desired tenderness, stirring occasionally. Serves 4 to 6.

If a plastic bag of brown sugar has hardened, try this. Add a dampened paper towel to the bag, close it and microwave for 20 seconds. Press out the lumps with your fingers. If that doesn't do the trick, microwave for another 10 seconds.

Cocoa Cappuccino Mousse

Stephanie Carlson
Sioux Falls, SD

Everyone will think you spent a lot more time than you really did on this quick & easy dessert.

14-oz. can sweetened
   condensed milk
1/3 c. baking cocoa
3 T. butter
2 t. powdered instant coffee
   or espresso

2 t. hot water
2 c. whipping cream
Optional: additional whipped
   cream, chocolate curls

Combined condensed milk, cocoa, butter and coffee in a saucepan. Dissolve instant coffee in hot water; add to pan. Cook over low heat, stirring constantly, until butter melts and mixture is smooth. Remove from heat; cool. Beat whipping cream in a large bowl with an electric mixer on high speed until stiff peaks form. Gradually fold chocolate mixture into whipped cream. Spoon into dessert bowls. Chill until set, about 2 hours. Garnish as desired. Serve 4 to 6.

Microwave Chocolate Pudding

Vanessa Dwyer
Ontario, Canada

So easy...you probably already have the ingredients!

2/3 c. sugar
3 T. cornstarch
1/3 c. baking cocoa

1/8 t. salt
2 c. milk
1/2 t. vanilla extract

Combine sugar, cocoa cornstarch and salt in a microwave-safe 8-cup bowl. Gradually stir in milk. Microwave on high for 10 minutes, stirring twice during cooking, until thickened. Stir in vanilla. Spoon into dessert bowls. Serve warm or chilled. Makes 5 to 6 servings.

Custard Rice Pudding

Edythe Bouquio
Vero Beach, FL

I always make too much rice. My husband just loves rice pudding and this is a great way to use leftovers! I combined a few recipes to come up with this one, and he loves it. The custardy top is delish!

2 c. cooked rice	1 t. vanilla extract
2-1/2 c. milk	1/8 t. salt
3 eggs	Garnish: cinnamon or
1/2 c. sugar	cinnamon-sugar to taste

Add cooked rice to a greased 2-quart casserole dish; set aside. In a small saucepan over low heat, bring milk just to boiling; remove from heat. Combine eggs, sugar, vanilla and salt in a blender. With blender running on low, slowly add warm milk and blend to combine. Pour over rice; sprinkle with cinnamon or cinnamon-sugar. Set dish in a large roasting pan. Carefully pour hot water into roasting pan around dish, filling halfway up the sides of dish. Bake, uncovered, at 350 degrees for one hour, or until a knife tip inserted in center comes out clean. Remove roasting pan carefully from oven; let casserole dish stand in hot-water bath until dish is easy to handle. Serve warm or chilled. Makes 6 servings.

Waffle sundaes! Just for fun, pour brownie batter into a well-greased waffle iron. Bake until crisp and serve, still warm, topped with ice cream, chocolate syrup and nuts.

Hot Fudge Ice Cream Sandwich Bars

Mel Chencharick
Julian, PA

This is a great way to make yummy ice cream sandwiches even better...your family will love them! I say this serves twelve, but most people take really big pieces and it only ends up serving nine!

16-oz. can chocolate syrup
3/4 c. creamy peanut butter
18t to 20 ice cream sandwiches
12-oz. container frozen whipped
    topping, thawed and divided

1 c. cocktail peanuts, finely
    chopped

In a microwave-safe bowl, microwave chocolate syrup on high for 1-1/2 to 2 minutes. Do not boil. Stir in peanut butter until smooth; let cool to room temperature. Line the bottom of an ungreased 13"x9" baking pan with ice cream sandwiches, cutting sandwiches to fit as needed. Spread half of whipped topping over sandwiches; top with half the chocolate syrup mixture and sprinkle with half of the chopped nuts. Repeat layers. Freeze for one hour before serving. Cut into bars. Makes 12 servings.

Happiness being a dessert so sweet,
May life give you more than you can ever eat.
– Irish Toast

EASY-AS-PIE
Desserts

Ice Cream Cake

D'Ann Kohls
Springfield, MO

This is my kids' favorite "cake." They request it every year
for their birthdays!

16-oz. pkg. chocolate sandwich
    cookies, crushed
1/4 c. margarine, melted
1/2 gal. vanilla ice cream,
    softened

11-3/4 oz. jar hot fudge sauce
8-oz. container frozen whipped
    topping, thawed

In a bowl, combine cookie crumbs with margarine. Press into the
bottom of an ungreased 13"x9" baking pan. Spread ice cream over
crust; cover and freeze until firm. Spread fudge sauce over ice cream;
add whipped topping. Cover; freeze until firm. Remove from the freezer
5 minutes before serving. Makes 12 servings.

Freezer Peanut Butter Pie

Joyceann Dreibelbis
Wooster, OH

A delectable no-bake dessert with two favorite flavors...peanut butter
and chocolate! A cool and creamy treat for the warm
summer months that is so easy to make.

1 qt. vanilla ice cream, softened
    and divided
9-inch graham cracker crust
1/2 c. creamy peanut butter

1/3 c. light corn syrup
Garnish: chocolate syrup,
    chopped walnuts

Spread half of ice cream into crust; set aside. Combine peanut butter
and corn syrup; spread over ice cream. Top with remaining ice cream;
drizzle with chocolate syrup and sprinkle with chopped nuts. Cover
and freeze for 3 to 4 hours. Remove from the freezer 15 minutes
before serving. Makes 6 to 8 servings.

Chocolate shavings for garnishing look so delicate but are
really simple to make. Just pull a vegetable peeler across
a bar of chocolate and watch it curl!

Spiced Apple Bundt Cake

Sue Klapper
Muskego, WI

I like to keep the ingredients for this smells-like-autumn spice cake on hand for those times I need to prepare a quick treat.

16-1/2 oz. pkg. spice cake mix
3 eggs, beaten

21-oz. can apple pie filling
Garnish: powdered sugar

In a large bowl, stir dry cake mix and eggs together. Stir in pie filling. Pour batter into a greased Bundt® pan. Bake at 350 degrees for 40 to 50 minutes, until a toothpick inserted near the center tests clean. Turn hot cake out onto a platter. When cool, sprinkle with powdered sugar. Makes 16 servings.

Easy Apple Pie Cookie Bars

Audra Vanhorn-Sorey
Columbia, NC

A family favorite...so easy, the kids can help pat out the dough!

16-1/2 oz. tube refrigerated
    sugar cookie dough, divided
1/4 c. sugar

4 t. cinnamon
21-oz. can apple pie filling

Press 2/3 of cookie dough into the bottom of a greased 9"x9" baking pan. Combine sugar and cinnamon in a small bowl; sprinkle 2/3 of mixture evenly over dough. Spread pie filling over dough. Take small amounts of remaining cookie dough, flatten slightly and place over the pie filling. Do not cover filling completely. Sprinkle with remaining cinnamon-sugar. Bake at 350 degrees for 30 minutes, or until cookie crust is done. Cool completely before cutting. Makes 12 servings.

A handy trick for greasing and flouring baking pans... grease the pan, sprinkle with flour, cover with plastic wrap and give it a good shake!

Pumpkin Bars

Kaela Oates
Waverly, WV

Similar to one of my favorite brownie recipes! Can't find pumpkin spice pudding? Use butterscotch for another yummy way.

15-1/4 oz. pkg. yellow cake mix
3-1/2 oz. pkg. instant pumpkin
    spice pudding mix

2 c. milk
2 c. butterscotch chips

In a bowl, beat dry cake and pudding mixes with milk until thoroughly mixed. Pour batter into a greased 15"x10" jelly-roll pan; sprinkle butterscotch chips on top. Bake at 350 degrees for 18 to 20 minutes. Cool; cut into bars. Makes 16 to 20 bars.

Pumpkin-Chocolate Chip Cookies

Christy Morrill
Liberty, MO

These cookies were popular at a craft fair our church years ago.

16-1/2 oz. pkg. spice cake mix
15-oz. can pumpkin

1 c. semi-sweet chocolate chips

In a bowl, combine dry cake mix, pumpkin and chocolate chips; mix well together. Scoop heaping tablespoonfuls of dough onto greased baking sheets. Bake at 350 degrees for 10 to 12 minutes, just until firm. Makes 2 dozen.

Keep cookies soft and moist. Tuck a slice of bread into the storage bag or cookie jar.

Very Lemon Bundt Cake

Darlene Ducharme
Lincoln, RI

*Really quick & easy! I love lemon desserts and this recipe
is moist and delicious.*

15-1/4 oz. pkg. golden vanilla
   cake mix
2 3-oz. pkgs. lemon gelatin mix
3/4 c. vanilla Greek yogurt

2 eggs, beaten
1-1/3 c. water
1 t. lemon extract

In a bowl, combine dry cake and gelatin mixes, yogurt, eggs, water
and extract. Beat until smooth; pour into a greased Bundt® pan. Bake
at 350 degrees for 43 to 48 minutes, until a toothpick inserted near
the center tests clean. Cool on a cooling rack. Serves 8 to 10.

Strawberry Poke Cake

Jill Burton
Gooseberry Patch

In a word...luscious!

18-1/2 oz. yellow cake mix
2 10-oz. pkgs. frozen
   strawberries in syrup,
   thawed

12-oz. container frozen whipped
   topping, thawed
Garnish: fresh strawberries

Prepare cake mix according to package directions; bake in a greased
13"x9" baking pan. Cool completely. With the handle of a wooden
spoon, poke holes halfway down into cake. Spread strawberries with
syrup evenly on top of cake; spread with whipped topping. Garnish
with fresh strawberries as desired. Cover and chill until serving time.
Makes 10 servings.

Substitute fruit juice for water in
packaged cake mixes for extra flavor.

EASY-AS-PIE
Desserts

Sugar-Free Punch Bowl Cake

Linda Trammell
Locust Grove, AR

One year, my daughter Tiffany made this dessert for my birthday. It was a hit with everyone! I am diabetic, and even I could enjoy it. So yummy! I sometimes use fresh fruit instead of pie filling.

2 1-oz. pkgs. sugar-free
  cheesecake pudding mix
4 c. milk
12-oz. container frozen sugar-
  free whipped topping,
  thawed

9-oz. pkg. sugar-free angel food
  cake, cubed
21-oz. can sugar-free cherry
  pie filling

Combine pudding mixes and milk in a large bowl; beat for 4 minutes. Add whipped topping; mix well and set aside. In a large punch bowl or trifle bowl, layer half each of cubed cake pieces and pudding mixture; add dollops of pie filling on top. Repeat layers. Cover and chill overnight. Makes 8 servings.

Oops! that's the way the cookie (or cake) crumbles! Turn a mistake into a luscious triumph. Simply layer in a trifle bowl with whipped topping and sliced strawberries or peaches, then chill.

Luscious Lemon Cream Cheese Pie
Heather Sinclair
Ontario, Canada

You'll love this light & lemony pie...perfect after a big dinner.

4.3-oz. pkg. cook & serve
   lemon pudding mix
2 eggs, beaten
1-3/4 c. boiling water
1/3 c. cold water
8-oz. pkg. cream cheese,
   softened

9-inch deep-dish pie crust,
   baked
Optional: lemon slices,
   whipped cream

Prepare pudding mix according to package directions, using 2 whole eggs, 1-3/4 cup boiling water and 1/3 cup cold water. Let pudding cool for 5 minutes. In a large bowl, beat cream cheese until smooth. Set aside one cup pudding. Gradually blend remaining pudding into cream cheese. Spoon into baked and cooled crust; cover and refrigerate 15 minutes. Spread reserved pudding over the top. Cover and refrigerate for 3 hours before serving. Garnish with lemon slices and whipped cream, if desired. Makes 8 servings.

When garnishing with lemon slices, do it with a twist!
Cut thin slices with a paring knife, then cut from center
to rind. Hold edges and twist in opposite directions.

EASY-AS-PIE
Desserts

Pink Twilight Cake

Sandy Ann Ward
Anderson, IN

*Just right for a baby shower, a spring luncheon or
even Valentine's Day!*

15-1/4 oz. pkg. strawberry
   cake mix
3 eggs, beaten
1 t. lemon extract

20-oz. can strawberry pie filling
Garnish: cream cheese icing or
   whipped cream

In a large bowl, beat dry cake mix, eggs and extract until well mixed.
Fold in pie filling. Pour batter into a greased 13"x9" baking pan. Bake
at 350 degrees for 30 to 35 minutes, until a toothpick tests clean. Cool;
frost with cream cheese icing or top with whipped cream. Makes 12 to
15 servings.

Cherry-Pineapple Dump Cake

Donna Jo Brown,
Peru, IL

*Not hing beats this recipe…simply dump in the ingredients, one after
another! This cake is a "must" at all Brown family functions.*

14-1/2 oz. can cherry pie filling
20-oz. can chunk pineapple,
   drained and 1/2 of juice
   reserved

18-1/2 oz. pkg. yellow cake mix
1 t. vanilla extract
1 c. butter, melted
1 c. chopped pecans

Spread pie filling in a greased and floured 13"x9" baking pan; top with
pineapple and reserved juice. Stir in dry cake mix and vanilla. Drizzle
butter over top; sprinkle with pecans. Bake at 350 degrees for 40 to
45 minutes, until golden. Serves 8 to 10.

If a recipe calls for softened butter,
grate chilled sticks with a cheese grater.
The butter will soften in just minutes.

Apple Pie Cake

Cathy Elgin
Saint Louis Park, MN

No frosting is necessary for this "eat-it-from-your-hand" cake.
The toffee bits provide a sweet crunch instead!

15-1/4 oz. pkg spice cake mix
1/4 c. oil
3 eggs, beaten

21-oz. can apple pie filling
8-oz. pkg. toffee baking bits

Combine dry cake mix, oil and eggs in a large bowl. Beat for 2 minutes with an electric mixer on medium speed. Add pie filling; stir by hand until mixed well, breaking up any large pieces of apples as necessary. Pour batter into a a greased and floured 13"x9" baking pan; sprinkle with toffee bits. Bake at 350 degrees for 35 to 40 minutes, until a toothpick inserted in the center comes out clean. Makes 12 to 15 servings.

Warm caramel topping makes a delightful drizzle
over baked apple desserts. Just heat it in the microwave
for a few seconds.

EASY-AS-PIE
Desserts

Beckie's Crazy Cake

Beckie Apple
Grannis, AR

I've been making this cake for years and so many times my friends will ask me, how'd you make this cake? But when I tell them, they don't believe me ! It'a light and very easy-to-make cake. I know you'll love it too!

18-1/2 oz. pkg. yellow cake mix
12-oz. can diet or regular
    lemon-lime soda
3-oz. pkg. strawberry or cherry
    gelatin mix

1/2 c. boiling water
1/2 c. powdered sugar

Combine dry cake mix and soda in a bowl. Use a fork to stir out lumps; do not overstir. Spread cake batter in a 13"x9" baking pan sprayed with non-stick vegetable spray. Bake at 350 degrees for 25 minutes, or until a toothpick tests done. Meanwhile, in a separate bowl, dissolve gelatin mix in boiling water; set aside. While cake is still warm, poke several holes in cake with a fork; spoon liquid gelatin throughout cake. Let cool completely at room temperature; sprinkle with powdered sugar. Makes 12 servings.

Cherry Funny Cake

Michele Coen
Delevan, NY

I love this recipe...it's really good! It is also delicious made with yellow or white cake mix and blueberry pie filling.

9-oz. pkg. chocolate cake mix
1/2 c. water
1 egg, beaten

9-inch deep-dish pie crust,
    baked
21-oz. can cherry pie filling

In a bowl, combine dry cake mix, water and egg. Beat for 2 minutes, until well mixed. Pour batter into baked crust. Drop pie filling by spoonfuls over cake batter. Bake at 350 degrees for 35 to 45 minutes, until a toothpick tests clean. Makes 6 to 8 servings.

Index

Beverages

Alan's Almond Tea Punch, 150
Carolyn's Slush Punch, 144
Green Tea Limeade, 170
"R" Family Punch, 154
Strawberry-Lemonade Punch, 171
Summertime Peach Punch, 170
Victorian Iced Tea, 137

Breakfasts

Biscuits & Gravy Casserole, 128
Cornbread Sausage Casserole, 128
Lizzy's Make-Ahead Egg Casserole, 129
Reuben Brunch Casserole, 130

Breads

Apple-Raisin Muffins, 14
Beer Bread Biscuits, 9
Boston Brown Bread, 12
Butter Biscuits, 31
Cheddar Corn Muffins, 38
Cheddar-Olive Bread Sticks, 17
Hasty Tasty Super-Moist Cornbread, 24
Quick Cheese Biscuits, 21
Southwestern Flatbread, 22
Sprightly Bread, 43
Tender Spoon Rolls, 31

Cookies

Aunt Betty's Pecan Squares, 180
Butter Brickle Cookies, 181
Cake Mix Cookies, 191
Double Chocolate Cookies, 190
Easy Apple Pie Cookie Bars, 210
Fuss-Free Strawberry Bars, 192
Gooey Butter Cookies, 190
Grape Jelly Granola Bars, 193
Macaroon Kisses, 193
Pumpkin Bars, 211
Pumpkin-Chocolate Chip Cookies, 211
Saltine Cracker Cookies, 181
Shortbread Fingers, 192
Speedy Peanut Butter Cookies, 180

Desserts

Angel Food Pineapple Cake, 186
Apple Pie Cake, 216
Aunt Patsy's Peach Pie, 202
Beckie's Crazy Cake, 217
Best Key Lime Pie, 177
Butter Pecan-Peach Cake, 183
Caramel-Cinnamon Dessert, 201
Caramelized Bananas, 205
Cherry Funny Cake, 217
Cherry-Pineapple Dump Cake, 215
Chocolate Eclair Cake, 178
Chocolate Pudding Cake, 189
Cocoa Cappuccino Mousse, 206
Custard Rice Pudding, 207
Daffodil Lemon Dessert, 199
Delicious Banana Toffee Pie, 186
Easy Berry Crumble, 185
Easy Chocolate Mint Pie, 197
Freezer Peanut Butter Pie, 209
Fresh Peaches & Strawberry Yogurt
  Sauce, 204
Frozen Cherry Dessert, 185
Grandma Carter's 5-Cup Salad, 198
Grandma's Butter Cake, 189
Grandma's Candy Bar Pie, 196
Hot Fudge Ice Cream Sandwich Bars, 208
Ice Cream Cake, 209
Joshua's Butterscotch Cake, 179
Lemon Custard Cake, 182
Luscious Lemon Cream Cheese Pie, 214
Malted Milk Ball Lover's Delight, 188
Microwave Chocolate Pudding, 206
Mississippi Mud Pie, 179
Mom's Strawberry Pie, 194
Momma's Pink Cloud Pie, 176
No-Guilt Fruit Fluff, 202
Oatmeal Crumb Dessert, 184
Orange Ice Cream Dessert, 198
Peanut Butter Cup Pie, 196
Piña Colada Cake, 187
Pink Twilight Cake, 215
Quick & Easy Rhubarb Pie, 203
Quick Apple Pie, 200
Quickie Pineapple-Cherry Dessert, 195
Raspberry & Peach Pound Cake, 195
Spiced Apple Bundt Cake, 210
Spiced Apple Crumble, 200
Strawberry Angel Food Cake, 182
Strawberry Poke Cake, 212
Sugar-Free Punch Bowl Cake, 213
Terrific Toffee Dessert, 197
Tropical Cheesecake, 177
Very Lemon Bundt Cake, 212
Warm Cinnamon Apples, 205

Mains

3-Ingredient Turkey Pie, 124
Aloha Chicken, 88
Baked Steak with Gravy, 115
Best Slow-Cooked Pork Ribs, 127
Busy Mom's Biscuit Cheeseburger Pizza, 133
Carnitas Pork Tacos, 100
Chicken & Gravy, 86
Chicken & Rice Casserole, 104
Chicken Mac & Cheese, 94
Chicken Reuben, 130
Chris's Spicy Mac & Cheese, 95
Country Smothered Chicken Tenders, 104
Creamy Ham & Beans, 92
Dad's Chicken & Noodles, 122
Delaware Chicken, 102
Delicious Beef Short Ribs, 97

Index

Index

Find Gooseberry Patch
wherever you are!

www.gooseberrypatch.com

Call us toll-free at 1·800·854·6673

U.S. to Metric Recipe Equivalents

Volume Measurements

1/4 teaspoon	1 mL
1/2 teaspoon	2 mL
1 teaspoon	5 mL
1 tablespoon = 3 teaspoons	15 mL
2 tablespoons = 1 fluid ounce	30 mL
1/4 cup	60 mL
1/3 cup	75 mL
1/2 cup = 4 fluid ounces	125 mL
1 cup = 8 fluid ounces	250 mL
2 cups = 1 pint =16 fluid ounces	500 mL
4 cups = 1 quart	1 L

Weights

1 ounce	30 g
4 ounces	120 g
8 ounces	225 g
16 ounces = 1 pound	450 g

Oven Temperatures

300° F	150° C
325° F	160° C
350° F	180° C
375° F	190° C
400° F	200° C
450° F	230° C

Baking Pan Sizes

Square		Loaf	
8x8x2 inches	2 L = 20x20x5 cm	9x5x3 inches	2 L = 23x13x7 cm
9x9x2 inches	2.5 L = 23x23x5 cm	Round	
Rectangular		8x1-1/2 inches	1.2 L = 20x4 cm
13x9x2 inches	3.5 L = 33x23x5 cm	9x1-1/2 inches	1.5 L = 23x4 cm